Your Retirement Lifeline

Dedication

This book is dedicated to my wife Olga who has been by my side for most of my retirement. While researching and writing my two 400 page family history books Olga was always nearby offering support and encouragement. Whether it was researching my mother's family in Minnesota, Wisconsin and Saskatchewan, or investigating my father's ancestry in Prince Edward Island and Cape Breton, Olga was always actively involved as we looked for one more piece of the never ending puzzle.

Jim & Olga

Olga displayed the same enthusiasm some ten years ago as we both tackled the book Get Up and Go, published by Dundurn Press. Olga came to my aid once more as I embarked on this last book Your Retirement Lifeline. Without Olga's positive presence not a word would have been written and I would not have had this opportunity to proclaim that this period has been the best years of my life.

Your Retirement Lifeline

Making It Better

By Jim McDonald

Disclaimer

The material presented in this book is for general informational purposes only. The reader should not substitute the content of this book for professional medical advice. If you need medical advice you should contact your doctor or another health care professional.

You are personally responsible for any actions you take as a result of using information in this book. If as a result of reading this book you participate in a sport or physical activity and sustain an injury or have any other problem, the author will not be held responsible.

Table of Contents

Chapter 1

Quality of Life is Attainable

Don't simply retire from something; have something to retire to.

Harry Emerson Fosdick

When you first retire you will rejoice in the realization that you don't have to get up for work in the morning; you are your own boss, you have no deadlines to meet, no one to report to and no meetings to prepare for. You will look upon retirement as the reward you have been waiting for. As you put your feet up and relax, you may say to yourself, "This is payback time and life is beautiful." That feeling of exhilaration is indeed possible, but to achieve it you'll have to work at it, because once you get that farewell handshake you're on your own.

Over five million Canadians (over 41 million Americans) now live in retirement, and surveys indicate that while most are enjoying life, some are less than satisfied, even despondent. Naturally, you hope to end up feeling good about your life in retirement and the intent of this book is to help you achieve that end.

Retirement will be new territory for you, with little resemblance to the working career you just left. This final phase of your life will be filled with new challenges and opportunities, so give it more than a passing glance; the odds are you will be in the retirement-zone for a long time, so get ready for it. Read books such as this one and talk to those who are already living in retirement. Work with your wife or partner to develop a game plan for a lengthy retirement, and then make every effort to make it happen. That's the way to lay the groundwork for a rewarding and successful retirement.

A Brief Retirement

Let's take a look at three major phases of an average person's life. Not too many years ago retirement years were short lived. Here's a depiction of retirement years compared to working years – back then.

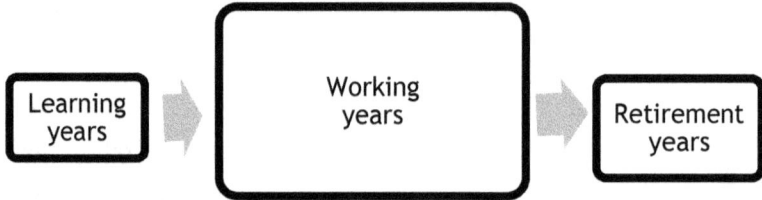

- Learning years consisted grade school, high school and possibly college or university.

- That was followed by a lengthy working career with retirement at age 65.

- Since a man's life expectancy was in the range of 70 to 75 years, retirement was confined to just a few scant years.

There were exceptions of course; my dad, born in 1884 lived for one month shy of 103 years.

Life expectancy at birth in Canada

- In 1930 males lived to age 60, females to age 62

- In 1950 males lived to age 66, females to age 71

- In 1970 males lived to age 69, females to age 76

- In 1990 males lived to age 75, females to age 81

- In 2000 males lived to age 77, females to age 82

- In 2012 males lived to age 78.8, females to age 83.3

Our life expectancy has gradually increased over the years until now it is commonplace to see people in their 80's doing such things as river rafting, skating and canoeing; unheard of just a few years ago. Why? Because many older people are healthier and in better physical condition than those who went before them.

Since we are speaking about the early years, let me mention a few Canadian events that have had an impact on retirement.

- In January of 1952 the Canadian Old Age Security benefits program was established. The Security pension was $40 per month or $480 per year for all men and women 70 years of age and over.

- In 1957 the Canadian Registered Retirement Savings Plan (RRSP) was introduced. Its purpose was to encourage employees to save for retirement.

- In 1966 Prime Minister Lester B. Pearson established the Canadian Pension Plan.

1/3 of Your Life Awaits You

With the average life expectancy now at 83.3 years for women, 78.8 for men, we are living longer than ever before.

You now have an excellent chance of living an additional one third of your life after retirement. Think of it; if you retire at 60 and live until 90 you have lived that extra third. Imagine living 30 additional years after your last day at work.

This is not pie in the sky thinking. With the advancements in medical technology we should all accept the idea that we may still be around at ages 90 or 100; like it or not. It's a bit scary and sure raises a lot of questions. Health issues will go hand in hand with increased age but many health concerns can be managed or prevented by your own efforts to look after your body. Above all, what you want to achieve is a high 'quality of life' during your later years.

Knowing that your retirement years may stretch well into the future should send you a strong signal that this final phase of your life deserves serious thought. With one third of your life at stake, you don't want to stumble into this period of your life unprepared, accepting whatever gets thrown at you.

A Lengthy Retirement

As a result of medical advances and other improvements, the retirement phase of our life is now totally new and different from what it was in the past. An evolution of significant importance has occurred.

The retirement phase of life has expanded to the extent that in many cases it lasts as long as our working career.

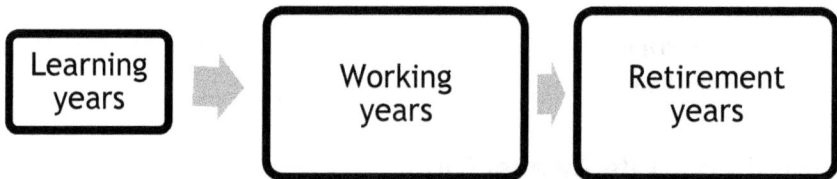

Learning years → Working years → Retirement years

We suggest that something called 'Quality of Life' should be a part of this prolonged phase of your life. Knowing that retirement may span two, or even three decades, retirees are now creating new careers during this period of their life. Many are returning to university or college, learning new skills, volunteering, or starting up a new business. In short they are making this a productive time of their life. Many are achieving satisfaction and even self-fulfillment from the new life they have carved out for themselves. As you proceed through the book you will see that if you make the effort, you too can inject Quality of Life into each important segment of your life. I hope you do.

What is Quality of Life?

Whether you are about to retire or are already retired, you should carefully plan your retirement with Quality of Life in mind. When

Governments conduct studies on Quality of Life, or the level of well-being of people in a sector of the country, they examine such factors as: the economy, climate, education, income levels, job security, gender equality and more. The factors that influence your personal well-being as a retired person are quite different.

When I began writing Your Retirement Lifeline I drew upon my own retirement experience (I have lived over 1/3 of my life in retirement) and the experience of others, to identify those factors which have a significant impact on a retiree's Quality of Life.

I decided that the following eight factors are essential to a successful and satisfying retirement, and these essentials are the focus of this book.

1. Enjoy your leisure time.
2. Take responsibility for the quality of your life.
3. Stay fit and healthy.
4. Eat right.
5. Be creative; find ways to boost your income if required.
6. Accept and manage change.
7. Don't smoke.
8. Acquire peace of mind in your later years.

The sequence of the above chapters is not intended to suggest any priority; each chapter is important in its own right. For example, the final chapter on Peace of Mind addresses several critical issues which become increasingly important as you age. I have placed it at the end of the book. It could just as easily have been placed first.

If, because of your individual situation you feel that we should have included another important factor, please keep that area of interest in your own mind as you proceed. We are not all alike and we certainly are not all exposed to the same influences on our life, so please make whatever adjustments are necessary to build Quality into every significant aspect of your lifestyle.

Quality of Life looks at how pleasurable and satisfying your retirement years are, not how many years you have lived. It's not how much money you have, but whether you enjoy the benefits of your money that count. It is not how many hours of free time you have in retirement, it's being able to make the best use of your time that is important. Below are some of the ways 'quality of life' has been described.

- The general well-being of an individual.

- One's ability to enjoy all that life has to offer.

- A person's ability to live a productive and happy life.

- The overall satisfaction a person gets from life.

Let me mention here that some folks, through no fault of their own may have a health problem or a disability that prevents them from attending to one or more factors that have an impact on their quality of life. This may prevent them from acquiring the quality of life in some areas that would otherwise be theirs. If this is your situation please be sure to read the paragraph under Health Problems in chapter 4, It's Your Life; You Make It Happen.

The Quality of Life theme finds its way into each Chapter because it applies to most areas of your life. As a side effect, quality in your life may increase your longevity; if that occurs consider it a plus.

Where to Find Q of L

Quality of life is free, and it applies to each of the eight areas mentioned earlier, and thus most chapters of the book. Although it is free, once you attain it, you become a much richer person with a better life. Acquiring Q of L requires effort on your part. You cannot buy it, you must earn it.

Studies have shown that the presence or absence of certain lifestyle factors will have a profound impact on our health and well-being during retirement. These three examples are of topics covered in the book.

- Exercise will often prevent or delay a disabling illness. If exercise is part of your lifestyle it will improve your quality of life.

- Eating Right will keep your waistline in check and also make you feel better about yourself; eating right will improve your quality of life.

- Getting your 'will' drawn up and into your safety deposit box will relieve you of that nagging anxiety and give you peace of mind. Taking that action will improve your quality of life.

Here's the bottom line: you want Quality in your life – because it will make your retirement better!

How enthusiastically you embrace each category will directly impact your Quality of Life and determine whether you live a rewarding lifestyle or a dreary, tired one with few rewards.

The ageing process is fraught with difficulties; our bodies are in a constant state of change so we must be ready to adjust and adapt to the ever shifting needs of our body. Today you may feel fit as a fiddle and tomorrow you may be laid up with a bad back or any one of a zillion ailments waiting to strike. Staying fit and healthy will do wonders to ease the transition as you move from 50 to 60 to 70 and beyond.

Make a Fresh Start

The moment you joined the ranks of the several million Canadians already retired you closed one chapter of your life and opened another. There is no going back. Let go of the past and move forward with confidence, as the future may be the best years of your life. It may take a few months to adjust to your new lifestyle and the reality of being retired, but if you aspire to do so, you will soon be living a meaningful and rewarding life. Most importantly, do not allow the past to taint your aspirations for an enjoyable and fulfilling future. Sure, for most people, there will be a period when you will miss the companionship of your fellow employees, the routine of the workplace, the sense of accomplishment, and that feeling of belonging to a group; but all of that is available within retirement. Your Retirement Lifeline will show you how to replace the void.

As you proceed through the book you will learn numerous ways to keep fit and healthy, socialize, and enjoy a sense of belonging, all at the same time. It also explains how you can acquire that all important sense of self-fulfillment during retirement.

Now that your working career has come to a close, you are free to make new choices with 'you' as the priority. With some 50 or more years of experience under your belt, you must know your aspirations and your priorities. With that in mind, now is the time to plan your future as you cross the threshold into your new life.

If you are not yet retired, prepare for the possibility that retirement may be thrust upon you at a time most convenient for your employer, not you. In 2012, the Royal Bank of Canada conducted a poll of Canadians aged 50-plus and found that 20% of retired Boomers had one month or less notice before their actual retirement, while 42% had less than six months notice before their compulsory exit.

If you entered the retirement arena unwillingly it may have caused you to feel bitter towards your employer or others; it may have led you to believe that you were all used up, put out to pasture, and of no value to anyone. Don't give in to that thought; your future may hold more promise than your past. Make no mistake about it, if you seek a quality driven, healthy lifestyle, your retirement years can be the most treasured time of your life. It has been said that many of us may attain the most fruitful years of our life between the age 50 and 75. I can attest to the fact that the 'here and now' can become just as enjoyable and rewarding as way back then.

You may become famous

- Ray Kroc began developing the McDonald's restaurant brand in 1954 when he was 52 years of age and struggling with diabetes and arthritis.

- Mahatma Gandhi led the famous Salt March in 1930 to protest the British tax on salt when he was 61.

- In 1852, Peter Mark Roget was 73 when he published his first edition of Roget's Thesaurus in London, England.

- John Glenn made his second flight into space in 1998 at age 77, thirty-five years after his first flight aboard the Mercury 6 space mission.

- Grandma Moses began to paint at the age of 76. She never had any formal art training but she painted every day, turning out more than a thousand paintings in 25 years. At the time of her death at age 101 she had paintings in museums as far away as Vienna and Paris.

- Michelangelo designed St. Peter's Cupola when he was 83 and remained active until he was 89.

Are You Recently Retired?

If you are just recently retired or not yet retired this may be the first time you have given serious thought to this phase of your life, so please take a few moments to think about the questions below. These questions will encourage you to think about the Quality of Life you envisage in your future lifestyle.

To help you focus, find a pen and paper and jot down your responses, for you may want to refer to your notes in the future. Better yet, you may want to enter your responses in a special notebook, because as you proceed there will be other occasions when you will want to make a note of your thoughts.

If you are not yet retired:

- What will you enjoy most about retirement?

- What aspects of retirement are you apprehensive about?

- What lifestyle adjustments will you have to make?

- As you see it now, what will be most important to you during your retirement?

Making Retirement Better

In future chapters you will also be asked to make a note of what you intend to do that will make your retirement better. By doing so, you will build up a source of valuable reference information for future use.

Chapter 2

Leisure is Good; Self-fulfillment is Essential

Rest is not idleness, and to lie sometimes on the grass under trees on a summer's day, listening to the murmur of the water, or watching the clouds float across the sky, is by no means a waste of time.

John Lubbock

Here's a quote from an article by Phil Hoefer, recently retired from the Colorado State Forest Service. *(Reprinted with permission from Phil Hoefer.)*

"Along with millions of others, I was raised with a strong work ethic. So strong in fact, that I now share an affliction with those millions where the idea of doing something simply for fun or relaxation often produces a terrible sense of guilt. Every time I try to do something just for fun this little voice in the back of my head constantly reminds me that there are more productive things I could be doing. Even now that I'm retired, I still can't completely shake the voice."

I too have a strong work ethic which hinders my ability to relax and enjoy; it even extends to my reading habits. For instance, when reading a crime novel, or a western, my little voice warns me that I should be reading something more cultured, something that 'will improve my mind'!

A lot of people have spent so much of their life working that they never learned how to have fun. Now is the time to make the change, for you probably have twenty or thirty promising years ahead of you. Quoting Phil Hoefer once more, here's what you must do:

"Identify those things that make your heart sing".

If you can do that you will be able to enjoy your leisure time for the rest of your retirement.

The Focus of this Chapter

- Leisure with a purpose

- Self-fulfillment is essential

- Your Project Search

- Stay engaged with life

- Manage your time

- Travel and Have Fun

Leisure with a Purpose

Imagine this; sleep until noon, watch television in the afternoon. It sounds enticing for the short term but destined for boredom. Leisure time or spare time does not imply constant lying about in some form of idle pursuit from dawn to dusk. It means spending time attending to a number of 'quality of life' imperatives, which were introduced in chapter one. If you fail to properly manage your leisure time you could encounter serious consequences down the road.

Here are some of the ways you should use your leisure time;

- Exercise and maintain an active lifestyle. Whatever your age, it is vitally important that you start now rather than later.

- Throughout your retirement you must attend to your financial affairs. If necessary, with the assistance of a financial advisor.

- Whether it is golf, hiking, or badminton, there is usually plenty of opportunities for social involvement at meetings, luncheons and casual get-togethers. Sometimes the social part is equally as important as the activity that brought you together.

- The Peace of Mind chapter deals with important issues that need to be addressed at this stage in your life.

- Each one of us need to acquire that all important sense of self-fulfillment which we deal with in the pages that follow.

- Hopefully at least part of your leisure time will be devoted to travel and fun.

So, leisure in retirement turns out to be more purposeful than the term suggests. And let's face it, every once in a while your leisure time will be interrupted by the need to cut the grass, fix a broken step, or change a light bulb.

What is Self Fulfillment?

When your heart sings as a result of something you are doing or something you have accomplished the Psychologists call it Self-fulfillment. Let's see what that means and how to achieve it.

From the dictionary:

Self fulfillment refers to the ability to make yourself happy and complete through your own efforts.

Self-fulfillment is unlike any of the other components that impact on your well-being during retirement. Self-fulfillment is a feeling that comes from within as a result of an accomplishment: it's a sensation, a feeling of exhilaration, a feeling of satisfaction which only occurs after you have personally accomplished something which you consider important and satisfying. Self-fulfillment is not a fleeting thing; when you think back to that event years later, that same feeling of fulfillment will come over you.

The accomplishment that generates self-fulfillment may be as gigantic as winning a gold medal at the Olympics or as minor as winning a blue ribbon for the best apple pie at a community picnic.

Here are two athletes whose exhilaration at the completion of their challenges must have been out of this world.

- Rosie MacLennan, a 23 year old trampoline gymnast from Toronto who won a gold medal for Canada at the London Olympics in 2012.

- Annaleise Carr a 14 year old from Walsh, Ontario, who completed a 52 kilometre swim across Lake Ontario on Sunday evening August 19, 2012.

Both Rosie and Annaleise put in years of practice, hard work and sacrifice in order to achieve their victory. And of course they must have experienced numerous smaller self-fulfillment moments as they climbed their ladder of success.

Here are two examples of self-fulfillment by everyday folks like you and me.

- Barbara took up painting when she retired. Today she put the finishing touches on another oil painting. She is proud of what she has accomplished, and so is her family. Definitely a self-fulfilling achievement.

- Bill, age 75, has been attending exercise classes at one of the city's Recreation Centres for three seasons. Today, as he walked back to his car after completing another class he felt pretty good about himself and his ability to stick with his exercises. Bill just experienced a sense of self-fulfillment.

Hierarchy of Needs & Self Fulfillment

Abraham Harold Maslow (1908 – 1970) was an American psychologist. He is best known for his Hierarchy of Needs motivation theory which he developed in 1943. His hierarchy is a description of the needs that motivate human behaviour and it still remains valid today.

As shown in the diagram below, Maslow proposed five different levels of human needs.

- Physiological needs: basic life needs such as air, food, drink, shelter, warmth, sex, sleep, etc.

- Safety needs: protection, security, order, law, stability, etc.

- Social needs: work group, family, affection, relationships, etc.

- Esteem needs: self-esteem, achievement, status, prestige, etc.

- Self-Actualization needs: personal growth, self-fulfillment, etc.

The hierarchy suggests that our most basic needs must be met prior to less basic needs; for example, a homeless person will seek food and shelter before affection or self esteem. Only when the lower order needs of physical well-being are satisfied will one be concerned with the higher order needs of personal development. As shown in the chart, self-fulfillment is one small part of the hierarchy at level 5, under Self-Actualization.

For many of us self-fulfillment is akin to nourishment in our lives; without it we would feel that our life had no meaning. When you retire for the night and your mind wanders over the events of the day you may ask yourself, "What was truly fulfilling about this day?"

Hopefully, you will occasionally feel a sense of fulfillment in having accomplished something worthwhile. If you never get that feeling of self-fulfillment or it is too infrequent, the rest of this chapter will help you identify how to get better acquainted with those things that will make your heart sing.

```
                    Self
                Actualization:
                 self-fulfillment
              Esteem Needs:
           achievement, status,
               responsibility
          Social Needs: family,
          affection, relationships
       Safety Needs: protection,
           security, order, law
      Physiological Needs:
   air, food, drink, warmth, sleep, etc.
```

Projects Generate Self-fulfillment

When you were in the workforce there was never a scarcity of work, someone was always telling you what to do. The problem was finding enough time to accomplish all that was expected of you. Now, in retirement the situation is reversed; nobody tells you what to do and you have so much time on your hands that it's easy to get bored. Granted – that's not everyone's dilemma but it is a problem for a lot of retired men and women who are still trying to figure things out. The big difference is that in retirement you choose what you want to do and when to do it. Sure, having total control over your life sounds exciting but it's also scary because it's not that easy to keep yourself motivated and wound up about life for the next thirty years when you're too old to do conventional work.

When it comes to self-fulfillment the challenge is no different than it is for fitness for health and happiness; you're on your own now, the onus is on you to search for answers.

As I present an approach to helping you resolve your (boredom) 'time on your hands' concern, I will not attempt to fill your day with trivial pursuits just to occupy your time, I will help you find meaningful and purposeful projects that will contribute to your quality of life and make your heart sing.

Working on the right Project will give you an opportunity to bring self-fulfillment into your life, not once but time after time.

Here is a 2012 quote from an article by Brian Crowley of The Globe and Mail, as he speaks about those over 65 who wish to continue working.

"Nearly half of Canadians of working age already expect to work beyond the age of 65, and not just for economic reasons, according to a survey done for one financial institution:

Nearly all of those who expect to work beyond age 65 cite one or more lifestyle reasons, including remaining mentally active, enjoyment of their jobs and the interaction with their co-workers." In other words, future retirees are coming more and more to realize that work is closely related to happiness."

Brian Crowley's article confirms what *Your Retirement Lifeline* advocates; retired men and women need to find ways to remain mentally active, interact with other people, and find self-fulfillment from within their retirement situation. Unless triggered by a financial need, there should be no reason to return to work or remain in the work force because that's where you can most easily chit-chat with your buddies. You can do all that in retirement too.

You cannot avoid the inevitable; retirement will one day become a fact of life, and you will find more happiness, enjoyment and contentment during this final phase of your life if, rather than resisting, you embrace and explore what it has to offer.

Throughout *Your Retirement Lifeline*, beginning in the first chapter I encourage retirees to 'Make a Fresh Start'. In this chapter I discuss numerous ways to meet people, socialize and enjoy life, and find self-fulfillment during your retirement years; including the idea of always having a project underway.

Allow me to interject a personal note; as I sit here working on this book (my current project) searching my mind for the precise word, trying to make each sentence convey the exact thought I have in mind, arranging and rearranging the flow of the content; my heart sings. I feel content and I am fulfilled. All of that, and I have no way of knowing if this book will ever see the light of day. In the meantime it provides me with something to look forward to each day and a reason to get up in the morning.

It's Your Time for Self-fulfillment

Take a moment to analyse your life by answering the following questions. If you answer 'yes' to one or more of the questions it's time to inject more quality into your life by seeking self-fulfillment.

- Am I bored with my life?

- Is each new day just another yesterday?

- Do I feel unhappy much of the time?

- Do I lack the energy and enthusiasm to do anything?

- Is my life gradually slipping away with nothing to show for it?

Searching for Your Project

While in the workplace you may have been fortunate enough to have a job where self-fulfillment was inherent in the process of doing your work. But now that you are retired you have to make an effort to search out such opportunities on your own, for they will not pop-up unless you initiate the action. In other words you have to be a 'self-starter'.

Here's a way to help you identify the type of project that will appeal to you. Take as long as you need to reflect on your past and come up with answers to the four questions listed below under the headings of: Talents, Skills, Wanted to do, Wanted to learn. Please retain your responses for reference so please enter them in your special notebook.

Talents: Make a list of your talents or abilities that make you unique as an individual. Natural talents can vary from music or athletic ability to a talent for working with people.

Skills: Make a list of your skills or those things you have learned to do. Skills will range from carpentry, cooking, teaching, writing, to computing.

One way to address this challenge is to think of it as finding 'new work' whether paid or unpaid. Consider making use of the skills you acquired during your working career to form the foundation for projects that will bring you self-fulfillment during your retirement.

- If skilled at research consider researching your family history.

- If skilled at carpentry consider making small items like bird houses, hobby horses, doll houses etc. for sale.

- If skilled at teaching, volunteer at a literacy organization.

- If you are a computer whiz, volunteer at a senior's community centre to teach seniors how to use a computer.

- If you like to work with your hands or have an artistic flair, you may enjoy Arts and Crafts. Try your hand at pottery, painting, stained glass, or woodworking.

Wanted to do:

Many of us can think of things we have always wanted to do but never got around to doing. Make a list of your 'wanted to do' yearnings. Some people find that retirement is an ideal time to begin a search of their ancestors. Others decide to volunteer, take up a hobby or write their memoirs.

Keep asking yourself:

- What do you enjoy doing?
- What do you want to get out of life?

Wanted to learn:

Thousands of adults attend evening or day classes to satisfy their desire to learn something new or pick up from where they left off years ago. If you have such a longing, now is the time to put it on a list. A retired friend in Nova Scotia is now learning to play the bagpipes; he just never had time before.

Once you have completed your four lists you may have an idea for a project. If so make a note of it.

Revisit Your Dreams

Think back to some of your unfulfilled dreams. Do you have a deep-seated yearning for knowledge in a specialty such as Astronomy, Ancient History or Archaeology? This may be your chance to sign up for a course at your local University or Community College.

You may have dreamed of building a model railroad system but never got around to it. You now have the time, so go for it! Or, take this opportunity to make new friends; join one of the many clubs such as Probus, Rotary, Kiwanis or Lions. Or you may prefer to join an outdoor club in your community where you will be able to have fun while attending to the physical needs of your body.

Project Examples

Here are a few examples of projects that some folks have pursued with passion and enthusiasm. Any one of them may trigger an idea for you. Let's face it, under different circumstances a project would be called work, but now that you have total control over when you work and when you take a stretch or a nap it turns into a fun thing to do. A project may last for a few days or the rest of your life.

Here are a few examples:

- Get involved in politics

- Get involved with a craft. Consider candle making, flower arranging, picture framing, quilting, stained glass, sewing, or woodworking.

- Go back to college or university:

- Join Toastmasters to improve your speaking skills.

- Learn about the stock market.

- Learn another language. I knew a lady whose first language was German, yet she studied Chinese after she retired. I have been told by a user that the Rosetta Stone language learning program is very good. Go to their website for a demonstration.

- The 'Centre for Extended Learning' (learning via the Internet) at the University of Waterloo has for many years offered degree courses to those over the age of 65 with no charge for tuition.

- Learn how to cook.

- Learn how to paint. My wife Olga began taking painting lessons shortly after she retired and she loves it. She began painting with acrylics but recently switched to oils. She finds it most fulfilling and we all love her finished work, some of which adorns our walls.

- Learn how to use the computer. You will usually find free classes at Recreational Centres in your city. In this day and age, using the

computer and email seems like the natural thing to do. Using the computer will keep your mind young and active and allow you to communicate with friends and family in distant places via email. The Seniors Guide to Computers is excellent; you can learn how to use the computer at no cost at - www.seniorsguidetocomputers.com.

- Learn to be a bird watcher. It will get you outdoors and provide you with exercise at the same time.

- Learn to fly an airplane.

- Learn to play tennis.

- Learn to play an instrument.

- Plant a garden in your own yard or somewhere else.

- Research your ancestors. I became heavily involved in family history research about 20 years ago and found it so fascinating that I ended up writing two 400 page books about my family ancestors; one about my father's family and one about my mother's family.

- Study photography.

- Study religions of the world.

- Take dancing lessons.

- Take up model railroading.

- Volunteer. There are so many places looking for volunteers: hospitals, food banks, nursing homes, libraries, parks, and literacy groups. I volunteered at a literacy establishment for a couple of years and found it most satisfying.

- Write a non-fiction book.

- Write a novel.

- Create a song collection. One of my sons has been collecting and saving music on his Play Station for several years. He has saved about 10,000 songs and his goal is 30,000. He gets his songs from a variety of sources: he borrows CDs from the library and friends, and then burns them onto his PlayStation. He also purchases MP3s from the internet. When finished he will have an enviable collection of rock & roll, blues, jazz, folk and classical music for his grandchildren.

Quickly now, make a note of projects you may like to pursue.

Stay Engaged with Life

Do you know anyone who is a borderline recluse, with no interests other than sitting at home watching television?

It's upsetting to even visualize someone living in such a state, but it happens. That lifestyle is not acquired overnight, it evolves slowly over the years and it's a situation we all hope to avoid.

Some years ago while spending the winter months in Florida I developed a routine of going for a walk through the community each morning. Others were doing the same thing, so as I met fellow walkers, there was a constant greeting of "Hi" or "Good Morning". One morning, as I approached an orange grove area I noticed an elderly man staring into the distance as he leaned against a fence post. Always ready to strike up a conversation, I approached him and said something like, "How are you doing?" He looked at me and said, "I'm bored". We talked some more and he reinforced the fact that he was depressed, lonesome and bored. I have always remembered that moment for it made me sad. What a waste! Here was a man who may have had a successful career, contributed to society, raised a family and now deserved his share of enjoyment and self-fulfillment during his retirement years. But somewhere along the line he had lost interest in life, had nothing to look forward to and no reason to get up in the morning. He failed to put 'Quality' into his retirement years. I hope you do better.

Three types of people

A Mrs. Butler is credited as being the author of the statement which says: There are 3 types of people.

- Those who make things happen

21

- Those who watch things happen

- Those who wonder what happened

I found it interesting to ponder Mrs. Butler's choices; to think back over my life and decide if and when I made things happen, how often I simply watched, and when if ever I was so withdrawn from the events of the day that I wondered what was going on. You may also want to spend a few moments doing the same thing. Of greater importance is where do you stand now?

Making things happen

When you retire, one of your primary objectives should be to stay engaged with life. You are now in a new phase of your life; don't hang on to your old identity from your working years. Begin fresh with new ambitions for your new life. I am not suggesting that you should attempt to emulate Ray Kroc, Mahatma Gandhi, or John Glenn, but you could strive to make things happen on a smaller scale, in your own community.

For instance, here are three examples from within my own condo building of people who in their own small way make things happen and improve the life of their neighbours.

- Jamie and his wife Donna, facilitate the 'Conversation Cafe' held twice a month, as residents get together to discuss topics of their choice.

- Olga has volunteered to keep our gardens looking beautiful for the past many years; by doing so she created an inviting scene for all who entered the property we call home.

- Our board of directors, who volunteer to manage the affairs of our condominium corporation, are primarily retirees who lead the way and make things happen on behalf of the residents.

I'm sure you can think of retired people in your community who still make things happen even though they are retired. You may be one of them.

Those who watch things happen

If you have reached the passive phase of your life there is nothing wrong with being a watcher during retirement. Just don't let yourself go to seed.

Read the newspaper, listen to the news on radio or television, talk to your friends and neighbours at every opportunity, stay abreast of current events, politics, the environment, and yes you should maintain a rudimentary knowledge of the electronic gadgets carried around by your grandchildren. That's the sort of thing that will keep you interested in life. It is impossible to keep up to-date on everything but you should make an effort.

You may ask, "What's in it for me, why should I clog up my brain with all that stuff I'm not even interested in?" For one thing, it will make you a more interesting person. You will be able to carry on a more intelligent conversation with more people and thus lead a more enjoyable life. It will also help keep you young. Keep your mind active; do crossword puzzles, read books and magazines, learn a new language, take dancing lessons, find something to write about.

Those who wonder what happened

When Mrs. Butler first penned these three lines I believe she must have added this last line with tongue in cheek, for I am not acquainted with anyone who consistently wonders what happened.

Who's your Confidant?

If you and your wife are both retired, why not nurture your friendship by arranging special little events each day such as going for a walk, enjoying breakfast together or watching the sun go down in the evening.

Always have someone you can talk to and confide in. If you have a partner, that's your obvious choice. If you don't have a partner or you and your partner seldom share, find someone else to fill that need. For us humans, it is essential that we have an opportunity to exchange thoughts, chat about trivialities, discuss how we feel, express our opinions, and periodically bare our soul to at least one other person. If you don't have such a person in your life, it may be that you should find one. The alternative could be a life of loneliness.

Imagine This

One fellow is so excited about life that he has a special name for each day of the week and he shouts it out to his family every morning. It goes something like this:

- Marvellous Monday
- Terrific Tuesday
- Wonderful Wednesday
- Tantalizing Thursday
- Fabulous Friday
- Stupendous Saturday
- Super Sunday

If you don't like these descriptions make up your own. I don't care for shouting at any time, especially first thing in the morning, but it may appeal to some boisterous folks. How about announcing, 'marvellous Monday' with a soft voice, a pleasant smile and a super hug for your partner.

Put Your Best Foot Forward

I spent my 35 year working career with Imperial Oil, initially in Saskatchewan and later in Toronto.

One year while working in Toronto, I was invited to join a team of line managers to conduct the yearly hiring interviews at Universities in Ontario. It was an interesting and rewarding experience; especially one interview which I will never forget.

This particular young man looked and dressed like most of the other students; it was what he said that shocked me. Early in our discussion he made these comments:

- *I don't know why I signed up to see you, because I know you won't hire me.*

- *I have poor marks.*

- *Nobody likes me.*

- *I'm not very good at anything I do.*

You guessed it; I did not recommend him for a second interview. This young man predicted that he would not get a job, and from the outset his behaviour ensured that outcome.

In this example, the young student failed his job interview because he purposely portrayed himself as a loser and nobody wants a loser on their team.

We don't always get what we want in life and more often than not, when we fall short, we never know what caused our misfortune. Why did you not get the job? Why was your wife angry with you? Why did you not get that apartment? Why did the taxi not stop for you? Why did the maitre d' seat you near the kitchen entrance?

The answer may be that, like the young student, you did not "put your best foot forward".

For most every occasion in life you need to behave, speak, dress and conduct yourself in a manner that is appropriate for the occasion and acceptable to those around you. If you refuse to do that, be prepared for some kind of rejection, however subtle it may be.

When I was in the army - 4 years of it - there was a full-length mirror on the wall near the exit of every barracks building. You were expected to check your attire before leaving, and if at some time later the Sergeant Major found something askew, there was nothing subtle about his reprimand or the consequences.

How we dress is important in our society. In recent years a more casual look has become the norm but there are limits. As seniors we should take the time to dress smartly every day of the week; it will bode well for our acceptance, our self-esteem and our self-confidence. No one wants to see us unkempt and scruffy; we owe it to ourselves to put our best foot forward. Check yourself out in your mirror. And, please don't wear that same old sweater for every occasion.

Manage your Time

Many retired people find themselves busier than ever. As they juggle their commitments they wonder how they used to find time to go to work.

Here are some basic time management guidelines. As you review them, remember that nothing is cast in stone, and you should allow yourself a certain amount of flexibility when it seems appropriate.

Make a 'to do' list – Each evening, make a list of your tasks for the next day.

Use a calendar – At an appropriate location in your home, maintain an up to date calendar where all your appointments are entered.

Prioritize - Some things you do are more important than others. And while two things may be of equal importance, one task may be more urgent than another. If your Visa payment is due today, that task is more urgent than getting your car washed, which can be done anytime. When you prioritize, you ensure that the important tasks get done first, leaving the less important for another day.

Establish a routine- If you have certain activities or tasks that must be done once or twice each week; try to arrange for these activities to occur at the same time and day each week. That will reduce the need to continually set new dates.

Be efficient - If some of your tasks for the day involve driving to several different locations, decide in your mind which place you will drive to first, second, and third, so that you will not be backtracking. This will save time, and money on your fuel costs.

Split tasks: Morning vs. Afternoon - Divide your to do list into two groups; morning tasks and afternoon tasks. A lot of retired folks prefer to take on the mentally challenging work in the morning while they are fresh, and keep the afternoon for doing chores that require more leg work and driving about.

Babysitting can be a pleasurable thing to do but sometimes these requests occur too frequently. As we age, many of us no longer have the energy required to care for the 'little darlings' who require constant vigilance. Looking after your grandchildren may also take up more of your leisure time than you want to spare. Learn to say no when necessary.

Travel

Travel often occupies an important component of our leisure time in retirement. Our purpose may be to visit relatives we haven't seen for some time, visit a city we haven't been to, take part in a theatre excursion to London, a golf trip, a walking holiday, a cruise, or a winter get-away to a warmer climate such as the Bahamas, the Caribbean or Mexico.

Enjoying yourself and having fun is a highly important component of retirement and we Canadians seem to find a wide variety of ways to do that. Some retirees spend most of the summer enjoying life at their cottage; others take pleasure from wintering in a warmer climate. Many more are addicted to exploring the sights, sounds and cuisine of distant cities. Then there is cruising, RVing, hiking and more. Wherever you are in the world you are likely to spot Canadian seniors doing what they love best.

While some folks travel far and wide, others with fewer resources will confine their outings to locations closer to home. Having less money does not mean that you cannot enjoy the small pleasures in life that make living worthwhile. A picnic held under a maple tree on the banks of a Canadian river, can be just as rich in love and happiness as that of another couple who share lunch at a luxury resort in Mexico.

Sometimes travel and social blend effortlessly together. That was the case when Olga and I joined a hiking group for a two week vacation on three separate hiking trips to France, Austria and Italy. As a group we stayed at the same hotel, ate dinner together and of course hiked together. I highly recommend hiking or walking trips, they are a lot fun, and you are not expected to do anything beyond your ability.

The accommodation will be good, meals exceptional and the hikes will take you to interesting and unusual areas. Check out these websites.

- Comfortable Hiking Holidays, in Toronto at - www.letshike.com

- Teachers Travel is at - www.teacherstravel.com

Wherever you end up, bear in mind you're still carrying around the same old body you had to care for back home. Soak up the atmosphere and live life to its fullest but don't ignore your health needs just because you are away from home.

It's a great feeling to return from a vacation with nothing but fond memories and interesting stories to tell. That's the way it usually is, but sometimes a combination of bad luck and poor planning intervene, and we return home with memories of misfortune and mishap.

Some come back with a stretched out waistline or back pain from too many hours behind the wheel of a car. Or the awful memory of an unexpected illness not covered by your insurance.

With all the excitement of preparing for your trip it's easy to get careless about protecting your health. If you look after your health at home it's even more important to do so while enjoying the sights in another part of the world. Here are a few important points to consider that will give you peace of mind.

- Learn about your destination before you leave.

- Get free travel reports from the internet.

- Check out Health Canada's Travel Medicine Program.

- Get vaccinations if required.

- Be sure you have adequate Health Insurance coverage.

- Be aware of Food and Water restrictions at your destination.

- Stay active after you arrive.

It's a good idea for you and your spouse to photocopy the photo page of your passport, your credit cards and other important cards; then each of you should carry both photocopy pages with you during your trip. If either of you lose a document or a card you will have information that will greatly assist in reporting the loss.

You expect to enjoy yourself all day, every day while on vacation. How about starting the day with a brisk 30 minute walk? If you normally do stretching exercises at home continue with your exercises while on vacation.

If you are looking for a reputable tour company I highly recommend Senior Tours, Canada. Their website is www.seniortours.ca.

If travelling by car

Stop for a stretch and switch drivers at least every two hours even if you think you don't need it. Sitting in one position behind the wheel of a car for an extended period contributes to fatigue, back pain, and stiffness throughout your body. Find a good location where you can safely pull off the road, take a short walk and enjoy a good stretch. Don't stop on the shoulder of the road unless it's an emergency.

Exercise when Flying

In recent years, even the airlines encourage their passengers to improve blood circulation by exercising during long flights. Passengers are encouraged to move their legs and feet for three to four minutes every hour and take periodic strolls down the aisle. These simple exercises are enough to prevent deep vein thrombosis (DVT), a condition caused by long periods spent in cramped conditions typical of the economy section of airplanes. Apparently, this sort of restricted movement can trigger illness when a blood clot in the leg breaks off and travels to the heart and lungs. Studies have revealed that DVT has caused the death of some long distance airline passengers.

It also pays to dress comfortably for long flights by wearing loose clothing. Remove your shoes and slip on a pair of soft slippers.

Making Retirement Better

Please consider each of the following questions, and then note your responses for future reference.

- What do you presently do that provides you with self-fulfillment; i.e makes your heart sing?
- If you don't have a project underway now, what will your next project be?

Chapter 3

Fitness for Health and Happiness

You have to stay in shape. My grandmother, she started walking five miles a day when she was 60. She's 97 today and we don't know where the hell she is.

Ellen Degeneres

A sk anyone over the age of fifty, "What's the most important thing in your life?," and I'll wager that most will respond with an unqualified, "My health!" The reason is simple, they want to live longer and enjoy life at the same time.

By the time you hit fifty you know damn well you have more years behind you than you have before you, so start paying attention to your health, it's more critical now than ever before. And now you have the time to do it.

You instinctively know that unless you're in good health, your joy of living will be greatly diminished. Some people simply trust to luck and hope for the best while others take steps that will lead to long-lasting health. This chapter will delve into details about how to achieve the Health and Fitness benefits that are so essential during retirement.

We will look at what exercises or activities you should do, how they should be done and how often. You may be surprised to discover how very little time it takes to keep your body in shape.

For some folks exercise may be an entirely new venture, but as we age, our bodies share a common need; a natural desire to move – to exercise, and once you hit retirement age the need to exercise becomes more important than ever. Even if you have never stretched a muscle, set foot in a gym or kicked a ball you will find exercise to be a rewarding experience, for it does more than increase your muscle tone; it helps you sleep better, improves your self-esteem, reduces stress levels, clears your mind, gives you better posture and balance, increases your energy levels, and enables you to get more enjoyment out of life.

The Focus of this Chapter

- Exercise

- Aerobics

- Flexibility

- Strength

- Find Your Niche

- Walking

Exercise Your Body

(Jim McDonald, Get Up and Go - Dundurn Press Limited, 2003)

When it comes to your body the old adage, 'use it or lose it' says it all. You already know that you may live a long time, so you have to figure out how to maintain your body's health throughout your life, however many years that may be. Bear in mind that everything you do will either improve or decrease your body's health.

If you have ever been confined to bed for a week or two you may remember how weak and rubbery your legs were when you attempted to stand up. That's what happens when you are inactive and don't use your muscles; they become soft and flabby.

Research shows that people who don't exercise lose 30 to 40 percent of their strength by age 65. When that happens, it becomes more difficult to carry out the normal functions of daily living. Even a short walk, getting up from a chair, or carrying groceries becomes a major chore. But it doesn't have to be that way. The experts tell us that most of our muscle loss occurs because we stop doing active things that require muscle power, not because we age. The good news is that regardless of age, you can strengthen your muscles by putting them to use.

Canadian personal trainer and kinesiologist Mike Bedard says, "Exercise is as close to the fountain of youth as it gets, and it only takes small changes in people's lifestyle to benefit from it".

A good workout plan should incorporate a mix of activities from each of the following three categories:

1. **Endurance or aerobic** exercises keep your cardiovascular system in good shape. The Mayo Clinic Family Health book describes an aerobic activity as one that requires your heart and lungs to function at an increased rate supplying your cells with more oxygen (aerobic means 'exercise with oxygen').

   Your main activity should be an aerobic exercise such as swimming, cycling, walking, hiking, skating, canoeing, x-country skiing and dancing. These activities improve the health of your heart, lungs and circulatory system.

   Health Canada recommends a minimum of 30 minutes of moderate exercise most days of the week. Brisk walking is considered moderate effort. Thus, you will benefit your health with as little as 30 minutes of moderate activity 4 days a week. What a bargain!

2. **Flexibility or stretching** exercises should be a part of any fitness program. Stretching or flexibility exercises prevent muscles from becoming short and tight. Activities such as bowling, yoga, curling, tennis, dancing, gardening, and house work all help to stretch your muscles. Flexibility exercises keep you limber and helps prevent falls. Once you have learned the techniques of stretching from a qualified instructor you can establish your own routine and stretch at home. My favourite reference book is Stretching by Bob Anderson. His book also provides specific stretching recommendations for those over fifty. Stretching exercises will go a long way toward preventing cramps and stiffness.

   If you are troubled with back problems, seek the advice of a health professional and you will find that certain stretching exercises can do wonders for your back.

3. **Strength or resistance** exercises will strengthen your muscles and help your bones stay strong. You need strong muscles to do the carrying, lifting, pushing, and pulling required to get through a normal day. Weight training is ideal for building muscles, but other exercises such as swimming, walking, hiking, and cycling will also improve your muscle strength. In other words, many activities fall under more than one category. In your search for ways to stay fit, consider adding weight training to your repertoire of activities to choose from. There is nothing intimidating about working out in a gym with other like minded men and women striving to accomplish the same goal.

Today, strength or weight training is considered an integral part of most well balanced fitness program. It is said that by age 75, one quarter of us can't even lift 10 pounds over our head. The next time you buy a 10 pound bag of potatoes, grab it in one hand and see if you can lift it over your head. Strength training helps our muscles stay strong and active.

If you decide to cycle you need strength to peddle your bike, if you take up canoeing or kayaking you will need strength to paddle. You want to be able to carry your own groceries and handle your own luggage on your next trip. Yes, muscles are needed for everyday living so don't let yours deteriorate.

While discussing active living with a group of adults one day, I asked what they did for exercise. Most responses were fairly typical but some confessed to leading a sedentary lifestyle, totally devoid of any kind of body movement. One lady's reply deserves mention here. She said, "I do my exercise first thing in the morning while I'm still in bed." That triggered a bit of a chuckle, but of course we knew she was talking about stretching. However good her intentions, this lady was not providing her body with a balanced workout, by limiting her exercises to stretching. She was depriving her cardiovascular system of aerobic activities, and without strength activities her muscles will deteriorate. There is nothing wrong with doing stretching exercises in bed as long as you acknowledge the need to do aerobic and strength exercises later on.

You may have heard the term 'weight bearing exercise'. It simply means an exercise in which your bones and muscles bear your body's weight during the workout. Thirty minutes of daily weight-bearing exercise such as walking, jogging or dancing, benefits not only your bones, but improves heart health, muscle strength, coordination, and balance. Prolong your independence with an active lifestyle that includes a balance of the three activity types: endurance, flexibility and strength.

Find Your Niche

(Jim McDonald, Get Up and Go - Dundurn Press Limited, 2003)

Early in your move to a more active lifestyle you should give thought to your exercise preference: solo, partner or group. Your decision will greatly influence the type of sport or exercise you choose. It will also have a bearing on whether you enjoy your new world of fitness, and your level of enjoyment will determine whether you continue to be active. Here are the three types.

Solo

Some activities like gardening are best done alone. Hiking, walking or cycling may be done solo, with a partner or in a group. If you live in a condo you probably have access to a small gym and a swimming pool where you can exercise solo whenever you wish, without having to concern yourself about others. One advantage of exercising alone is that you can pick your own time and place, and enjoy privacy while exercising. But there are disadvantages to exercising alone:

- You will lose interest more quickly and may quit.

- You don't have an instructor's input on the correct way to perform an exercise.

- You have no interaction with other people. If even a small part of your reason for becoming active was to have additional social contact, try to find that social contact in the activities you select.

Partner

If you are married, have a partner or close friend, try to get him or her involved, but if your partner is not interested don't let that hold you back. Many men and women are extremely active in physical fitness activities while their spouses pursue some other endeavour. Don't deny yourself of something you want to do just because your partner has other interests. If your partner has never shown any interest in exercise and is emphatic about not wanting to become active, don't delay; look after your own health by becoming physically active on your own.

Jim & Olga

Group

Whatever the activity, there's energy in a group. There is a certain enthusiasm generated within a group and it's catching. You will work harder and longer in a group than you will alone.

Here are a few advantages of exercising in a group:

- By attending an instructor led group exercise class you learn how to exercise. If you are not accustomed to exercising this is a must, for if exercises are not performed correctly they can do more harm than good.

- When you join a group exercise class it is usually a commitment of one or two days per week and you are more likely to attend.

- Exercising is more fun when you are with a group.

If you get some of your exercise through a sport such as cycling, hiking, or kayaking, that sport takes on added value in a group. You still get your exercise, but in addition you have social contact with like minded people. In a group there is always a fun atmosphere and a sense of sharing which adds pleasure to what you are doing.

Range of Effort

In the world of physical activity you will sometimes find the terms Light, Moderate and Vigorous used to describe the amount of effort or work required to carry out an activity.

Light Activities such as slow walking or bowling require less energy and effort, thus you must spend more time doing the activity in order to gain the same health benefit as one doing the activity at a moderate rate. Health Canada's recommendation of 30 minutes of moderate exercise becomes 60 minutes when performed as a light activity.

Moderate activities call for more effort and therefore require less time than the same activity performed with a light amount of effort. Therefore 30 minutes of brisk walking, riding a bike, raking leaves, water aerobics, and swimming or dancing most days a week meets the Health Canada's recommendation.

Vigorous activities that make you breathe hard and perspire require only 20 to 30 minutes a day i.e.: aerobics, jogging, hockey, basketball, fast swimming, and fast dancing.

You can mix and match your activities. There is no right combination, as long as you meet the minimum times for the intensity you have chosen. Hopefully you will feel so good you will choose to do more than the minimum.

A minimum of thirty minutes a day, four days a week sounds easy enough. And those 30 minutes do not have to be done all at once. Three 10-minute segments of moderate activity at different times during the day count for 30 minutes of activity. Nearly half of us don't do that much for our health.

If you are walking for the purpose of improving your health, ask yourself if you are using enough energy to benefit your body. If you notice that you are walking slowly, gradually pick up the pace. The key word here is 'gradually'; don't push yourself too hard when you begin a change in your level of activity.

London's Bus Driver Study

In 1949 Jerry Morris a London epidemiologist (a branch of medicine that studies epidemics) was the first person to unintentionally discover a great truth about health; that there is a connection between physical activity and improved health.

Here's how the bus study came about.

Jerry had been engaged to conduct a study whereby he compared London's, double-decker bus drivers with the ticket takers (conductors) on the same buses.

He discovered that the ticket takers walked about 500 to 750 steps each working day as they climbed up and down the stairs of the double-decker buses. In the meantime the bus drivers sat behind the wheel driving the bus. Thus the ticket takers were active all day long while the drivers spent all day in a sedentary position.

Jerry's research showed that the sedentary bus drivers had double the risk of heart attack than the more active ticket takers. This health difference was of course attributed to exercise. Today, almost everyone understands that physical exercise can help prevent heart disease, as well as cancer, diabetes, depression and much more. But on that day in 1949 when Morris looked at the bus data, he was the first person to see the link between exercise and good health.

Note: For years I assumed that today's adults were all aware that physical activity improved one's health, but I was wrong. Just last week while speaking to a 60 year women who was attending a rehab program following a heart attack I asked her, "Do you find the rehab program helpful?", and she promptly responded, "Yes it's great, but mainly I have learned that exercise is important to my health. I never knew that."

Canadian Health Measures Survey

In 2010 the outcome of the Canadian Health Measures Survey was published. Below are a few excerpts of the disappointing results of that study. But first, here is a quote from the introduction:

"The numbers are so startling that they should cause everyone to sit up and take notice. We should all question our own situation, do a self-evaluation of our lifestyle and take whatever action is necessary. Most certainly we do not want to end up being overweight or obese between the ages of 60-69 or any age for that matter"

Excerpts from the report:

- For females 65 years of age or older, only 37.7% were moderately active.

- For males 65 years of age or older only 50% were moderately active.

- Adults spend an average of 9.5 hours a day in sedentary pursuits, or approximately 69% of their waking hours.

- On the basis of their waist circumference, 65% of women and 52% of men aged 60 to 69 were considered to be at high risk for health problems.

This report is available on the Internet.

Do It Now

If you are inactive now and remain so until next year you will be one year older with nothing to show for the year gone by. For every year you continue to be inactive the more difficult it will be for you to get your body back to where you want it to be.

Remember that once you hit 50 or more, active living is not something you do in the short term; you must embrace it for the long haul. Active living is something you must aspire to for the rest of your life, and with each new birthday it becomes more important than it was before.

Getting Started

Once you decide to get active, start moving right away. Don't ponder and analyse the heck out of anything. Just do something.

If you already know what sport or activity you want to get into, that's great; so start riding your bike, going to the gym, playing badminton or whatever. If your selected activity requires attending a group class, but the commencement date is not for a few weeks, don't lounge about doing nothing in the meantime, select another activity such as walking and get going without delay while you are motivated.

Think back to a sport like skating, swimming or cycling you enjoyed as a kid, you may want to try that same thing again. You want to have fun and enjoy your new active lifestyle so don't get into something that you will find intimidating or overly strenuous. Whatever you choose, don't hesitate to switch to another activity if something else turns up that holds more appeal. Remember, your objective is to keep healthy by living an active lifestyle.

I remember quite clearly the day I decided to choose canoeing as a way to stay active and mingle with other like minded enthusiasts. A couple of months after my heart bypass surgery I was in Florida, out for a morning walk when it occurred to me that, in addition to my constant solo walking I should search for an activity that would not only keep me active but provide interaction with other people. After a bit of mental brainstorming I recalled that a few years earlier I had enjoyed canoeing. That was it; as soon as I returned home I searched through the yellow pages, made several phone calls and joined the 'Seniors for Nature Canoe Club' in Toronto.

My wife and I remained active members for 20 years. We always returned from our outings feeling tired but happy at having had the privilege of spending a fun filled day with a great bunch of men and women with similar interests. Once you get the urge to do something in your best interests, follow through to bring your idea to fruition.

(Jim McDonald, Get Up and Go - Dundurn Press Limited, 2003)

Where Do I Start?

By Elie Wiesel

But where do I start?

The world is so vast,

I shall start with the country

I know best, my own.

But my country is so large.

I had better start with my town.

But my town, too, is large.

I had best start with my street.

No: my home. No: my family,

Never mind, I shall start with myself.

Ideas for Getting Started

- Before beginning an exercise program, discuss your plans with your doctor, or other health professional.

- If you have not exercised for some time, don't overdo it. One of the most frequent mistakes people make is taking on more than they can handle.

- Don't hesitate to start off by joining a group involved with one of the gentle sports like lawn bowling, yoga for seniors or walking.

- One safe way to get started is to join an exercise group at a community centre where you will have a lot of support from like minded people.

- Join an outdoor club.

- Select the time of the day that will fit best with your normal routine. I always like mornings because I can get my exercise looked after before a lot of other things clog up my day.

- It's better to choose one activity and stick with it than select two or three, then drop-out before you have even worked up a sweat.

- Wear appropriate clothing for the weather and type of activity. For walking, you need comfortable running/walking shoes. Two or more layers of tops are better than one heavy jacket. That way you can remove one layer if you get too warm.

- Try to hook up with a friend; if your spouse will join you that's even better.

- Eventually you should develop a regular exercise plan for your activities.

Once you have completed a few outings or activities you will feel better, more refreshed, more energetic and proud of yourself. Store those wonderful feelings in your memory bank; and call them to mind when you need motivation to get going at some time in the future.

Walk for Your Health

Haven't exercised in some time? That's no problem. Start off slowly with a 15 to 20 minute walk. Increase your pace and your time gradually over a period of 2 months until you are walking briskly for a total of at least 30 minutes four days a week. It will lift your spirits and brighten your day. When you step out your door you can walk the sidewalks in your area, along river trails, on bike trails, nature trails, and public parks where you can enjoy the sights and sounds of the great outdoors. Make walking a more enjoyable experience by inviting others to join you.

You can join a group of mall-walkers and do your walking indoors during the winter months before the stores open. When you do a mall walk, find a set of steps that you can add to your normal routine. Steps are a great way to build up your leg muscles.

Walking is the favourite activity for 70% of our adult population. Surveys show that while most people chose walking as a physical activity, many of us need to walk a bit faster to achieve the maximum in health benefits. Wear good quality, comfortable running/walking shoes that provide good support and don't cause blisters. Always bring along a bottle of water and drink it liberally, especially in hot weather. There are some neat carrying devices on the market that fit onto your belt for carrying your water bottle.

With walking, you can set your own schedule and do it anytime. You can walk alone, with a partner or with a group. Best of all it doesn't cost anything and it's virtually injury-free. If you're in good shape you probably walk about 6 km in 60 minutes. That's a brisk pace. If you are in the 65-plus age group, your pace may have decreased to around 4 or 5 km in 60 minutes, which is still a respectable clip.

Years ago when I and thousands like me walked and walked around the track at the Toronto Rehab Centre after heart surgery we knew exactly why we were there and it wasn't for a walk in the park. It was to improve our cardiovascular fitness. Walking is an aerobic exercise that gets the heart beating faster so that it transports oxygen-rich blood from the lungs to the muscles. Walking is also at the core of rehab treatment for many ailments besides heart problems.

Walk Smartly

It is said that walking is something you can do without any lessons, but when you see some folks ambling along I suspect they could benefit from my Dad's counsel: stand up straight – pull your shoulders back – walk smartly – and pick up your feet; that's what he used to tell us kids. When you walk, allow your arms to swing naturally and let your hands, arms and shoulders relax.

You should know how fast you walk so that you can establish your goals. Drive your car for a distance of say, two kilometres. Later, walk that exact same location and distance and record how many minutes it takes. You can now calculate your walking speed in minutes per kilometre or minutes per mile. One easy way to tell if you are walking too fast is to do the 'talk test'; if you are unable to carry on a conversation with your partner you are walking too fast or too strenuously. Always pay attention to how you feel both during your walk and the next day.

Walking briskly is just as beneficial for your overall health as running, but without the negative side effects. When you walk briskly on a regular basis, it can reduce your blood pressure; increase the efficiency of your heart and lungs, and burn excess calories. Walking is an enjoyable, fun thing to do; it will make you feel better about yourself, improve your attitude and increase your energy level.

Why Do I Walk?

By Ed Cunningham

Pantin like a pack mule, sweatin' up a storm,

Keeps me youthful, keeps me loose,

Tightens my tummy, and shrinks my caboose,

Why do I walk? 'Tain't no mystery ---

Wanna have a good medical history.

Doctor told me walkin' is great--

Helps them blood cells circulate.

Great for the lungs, great for the ticker,

Can't nothin get cha in better shape quicker,

Feels so healthy, feels so sweet,

Pumpin' my arms and flappin my feet,

Moldin' my muscles, firmin my form,

beats bein lazy---

Why do I walk? Maybe I'm crazy!

Love my Pedometer

The pedometer is an inexpensive device which measures how far you walk or jog. It is usually worn clipped to a belt or waistband and responds to the motion of your hips each time you take a step. Hikers, walkers and joggers usually have their pedometer set to display distance in either miles, kilometres or steps; and it will even calculate the calories you burn. Your pedometer does all the work; all you have to do is remember to push the Start button at the beginning of your outing.

When you purchase your first pedometer it's important to follow the instructions provided and accurately set your stride and weight so the pedometer can calculate your distance travelled and calories burned. Later on it's a good idea to check the accuracy of your pedometer reading against a known distance such as a walking track or a distance measured on the odometer of your vehicle.

As you might expect, there is now an App for that. That's right, if you do a search on the net you will find numerous Apps for walking or jogging which you can download onto your iphone. They will not only record how far you walk or jog, but will record numerous other data you may or may not be interested in. Some will even talk to you like GPS. Some Apps are free, some cost money.

A growing number of people are measuring the distance they walk during a normal day, with a goal of 10,000 steps which is equal to about 5 miles or 8 kilometres. Someone in Japan came up with the idea several decades ago and it has caught on around the world. It's just another way to keep you interested in exercise with a fun kind of goal.

In Canada, men average about 9,500 steps a day, and women walk an average of 8,400 steps per day. In the 60 to 79 age group, the daily average is much lower at 7,900 for men and 7,000 steps for women.

Making Retirement Better

- Is your present level of physical activity sufficient to maintain your fitness as you grow older?

- What type of exercise or physical activity do you do?

- Do you engage in moderate physical activity for a minimum of 30 minutes 4 days a week?

- What specifically, do you intend to do in the area of fitness and health that will make your retirement better.

Please make a note of your responses in your special notebook.

Chapter 4

It's Your Life; You Make it Happen

Opportunity does not knock, it presents itself when you beat down the door.

Kyle Chandler

No one will come knocking at your door or send you an invitation to join a venture guaranteed to improve your health and your outlook on life. It's not going to happen so don't wait. You must take the initiative; you have to make it happen. If you are waiting for a more opportune time to start doing something about your inactivity, don't wait for that either, because there will never be a perfect time - your best time is now. As someone once said, "It may not be your fault that you are down, but it's your duty to get up."

The Focus of this Chapter

- Make exercise a way of life.
- Make your health last.
- Stay motivated.

If you choose to remain inactive, your bone strength will decline, your muscles will get weak, and you will lose flexibility in your joints, tendons and ligaments.

Not too long ago a Toronto Star headline said this:

We're living the easy life and it's killing us. Increasingly idle, we're becoming increasingly big --- and less healthy.

If you are already retired you are in a most precarious position for you don't even go to work anymore; the temptation to assume the sitting position is all around you. You have to fight off the natural tendency to become inactive. You must find a way to join the retired men and women who live an active lifestyle. Once more, Health Canada cautions us that if we remain inactive, we run the risk of:

Premature death - Heart disease – Obesity - High blood pressure – type 2 diabetes – osteoporosis – stroke – depression – colon cancer.

If you're beginning to feel uncomfortable with your sedentary lifestyle, totally devoid of physical activity, huffing and puffing at every turn, pause and ask yourself, "When was the last time you felt really great?" Could it be that you have forgotten what if feels like to have a zest for life, be full of energy, bursting

Hiking with the Club

with enthusiasm? Don't blame fatigue on age even if you've hit 60, 70 or more. Old and tired have more to do with attitude, outlook and lifestyle than the calendar.

If you maintain your health, retirement can be an enjoyable period in your life. Your children have grown up and left the nest and you are now free to do all those wonderful things you never had time to do before. But there is always that nagging concern about health. Of what value is a long life or an abundance of money if health problems remove you from the pursuit of a pleasurable life? Especially if your health problems were brought about by inactivity; something you have control over.

During Roman times life expectancy was a mere 25 years. Today as a Canadian you may live for another two or three decades and it will be a challenge to keep your body fit enough to enjoy all those extra years.

Make Exercise a Way of Life

A few years ago while speaking to a young woman who jogged thirty minutes every morning before breakfast; I asked her, "How do you maintain the motivation to keep at it every day?" She responded by saying, "Jogging is just as much a part of my morning routine as brushing my teeth." That's the way we should look at active living. It should become as natural as any other part of our daily life. If you enjoy going for a 30 minute bike ride or a 30 minute brisk walk every morning, make it part of your regular routine; give it the same priority as your morning newspaper and coffee.

Examples of indoor activities:

Badminton, Basketball, Volleyball, Bowling, Curling, Senior hockey,

Swimming, Mall walking, Aqua Fit, Group fitness classes.

In most communities you will find both city owned and privately owned facilities anxiously waiting to help you shape up and stay healthy. Some will be equipped with a hockey rink, swimming pools, squash courts, tennis courts, and much more. Many will offer custom designed exercise training and some will include group fitness classes. All will be staffed with highly qualified instructors. Costs will vary from just a few dollars a year at a Senior Centre to a few hundred at a private fitness club.

Check the Yellow Pages, City Hall, your local newspaper, and the Internet for information about what's available in your community. Remember, you don't have to join a fitness club to stay in shape, there are plenty of alternatives. You are not striving for bulging biceps, killer abs or great gluts; you just want to stay physically fit. You can accomplish that by walking, hiking or cycling and it won't cost you a cent.

The YMCA

You may have a 'Y' in your city. If so check it out as a place to go for indoor fitness. They usually offer a wide range of facilities such as swimming, group fitness, weight training and recreational sports such as basketball, soccer and martial arts.

Senior Centre's

Call them what you will, there are numerous Seniors Centres, Community Centres, Recreation Centres and Older Adult Centres across Canada that act as a gathering place for men and women age 55 or older.

Their schedule usually includes programs in education, recreation, health & wellness, and special events. All of this is available for a token membership fee and a small charge to take part in special programs.

I used to discount Senior Centres as a place where frail old folks shuffled from the bridge table to the bingo hall, but no longer. Today's Senior Centres offer a variety of top notch fitness classes conducted by qualified instructors. They offer group fitness activities such as stretching, aerobics, line dancing, ballroom dancing, yoga, tai-chi, Pilates and much more.

Their instructors put enthusiasm into their sessions and make you feel like part of the group as you sweat and stretch your muscles from your neck down. Instructors don't force you to do more than you are capable of.

You should recognize your own limitations but your instructor will encourage you to heed the warnings of your body. Their programs incorporate a mix of all three activity types into a one-hour group workout. A typical one hour session may be: 10 minutes to warm-up, 30 minutes for the main aerobic activity, with the final 20 minutes allocated to strength activities, stretching, and cool down.

If you are looking for physical activity that benefits your health you'll find it in spades at these centres. Give them a try.

In Your Condo

If you live in a condominium there may be a small gym right in your building. If so, there will be treadmills and stationary bikes just waiting for you to give them a try. If you live in a high-rise condo try using the stairs as a built-in exercise pathway. Walk up one flight of stairs, then along the corridor to the end of the hall, up another flight of stairs, down the hall and up another flight of stairs and so on. If you do that a couple days a week you will give your heart and circulatory system a good workout. You will also strengthen your leg muscles.

Examples of outdoor activities:

Canoeing, Hiking, Kayaking, Rowing, Soccer, Tennis, Walking, Snowshoeing, X-country Skiing.

You can find outdoor clubs in nearly every town and city across Canada. Most clubs have been in business for many years and have well established programs and procedures with organized outings and competent leaders. Members operate their own club, so once you become qualified; you too can become a leader and possibly a member of the executive. As previously mentioned, my wife Olga and I were active members of The Seniors for Nature Canoe Club in Toronto for some 20 years. Like most clubs, the SFNC also promoted hiking, cycling and X-country skiing

The way I see it, joining an outdoor club is the way to go.

Gardening

Yes, gardening is a popular physical activity for Canadian adults. In fact it ranks up there with walking and it's easy to understand why.

Gardening is an exercise that allows you to combine fresh air and sunshine with enjoyable, productive work. While you do all that digging, planting, weeding, watering and raking you strengthen your arm and leg muscles and build strong bones. But yard work is physically demanding so ease into it at the start of a season so you don't strain your back and shoulder muscles. If you don't have a garden of your own, you may want to look into other options such as joining a group of gardening volunteers. Most communities have these groups who attend to gardens at such places as seniors' homes.

Keep moving every day

- When you park at a shopping mall, don't search for a spot near the entrance, park where you are forced to walk a couple minutes to the mall entrance. Don't always drive your car for those short trips to the corner store; walk and it will benefit your health.

- If your goal is to lose weight or simply get into better physical condition, have patience. It took years of over eating to add that weight and years of inactivity to lose your strength, so train your mind to appreciate your small daily gains and your long term goal will take care of itself.

- If you normally use the bus, get off a couple stops before your regular one and walk the rest of the way. In the subway or shopping mall, take the stairs not the escalator.

- If you live in a condo or apartment, don't always use the elevator; take the stairs once in a while.

- Get up from whatever chair you are in and do some stretching and bending every hour or so.

- While moving your body – as in walking – focus your mind on your body and how it feels. Think about how fortunate you are to have a working body that moves with ease. Not everyone enjoys that luxury.

Health Problems

Some Canadians are limited in the type and amount of exercise they can do because of a physical condition or health problem. If you are in this situation, ask your doctor if there is an exercise program designed for your particular need.

There are numerous safe exercise classes for people with conditions such as: osteoporosis, multiple sclerosis, Parkinson's, chronic obstructive pulmonary disease (COPD), arthritis, fibromyalgia, back pain, recovery from injury or surgery, and more.

Many cities have warm water Therapeutic Pools with qualified aquatic trainers who can help.

Make Health Last

In 2013 the Heart and Stroke Foundation launched a program called "Make Health Last". As part of their program an impressive and startling mix of video and text flashed across the TV screen. It scared the living daylights out of me, but it does get the message across. Here's what it said:

What will your last 10 years look like? On average we'll spend our final 10 years with sickness and disease.

Then the message told the viewer:

"It doesn't have to be this way. The good news is that you have the power to change your future. Assess your risk for heart disease and stroke, and you'll take the first step toward a healthier future."

The Heart and Stroke Foundation also released the results of a Canadian survey conducted in 2013. Here is what they found:

- 85% reported not eating enough vegetables and fruit.

- Over 40% said they are not as physically active as they should be.

- 21% smoke.

- 11% are heavy drinkers.

- Almost 30% feel they are often or always stressed out.

This should cause boomers a lot of concern," says Heart and Stroke Foundation spokesperson Dr. Beth Abramson.

"The good news is that if lifestyle changes are made now, many Canadians can considerably reduce the effects of heart disease and stroke. It is possible for us to take charge of our heart health, reduce hospitalizations and immobility, significantly improving the quality of our lives."

According to the Heart and Stroke Foundation, Canadians have the power to *Make Health Last* and shrink the 10-year gap between how long they live and how long they live with health. Here are the five controllable behaviours.

- Physical inactivity results in nearly four (4) years of quality life lost.

- Eating a poor diet equals nearly three (3) years of quality life lost.

- Excessive stress can cost nearly two (2) years or more of quality life lost.

- Quitting smoking can add over two (2 1/2) years of quality life.

- Excessive drinking costs Canadians (2) two years of quality life lost.

Charlie's Justification

Charlie's inclination to rest was stronger than most, and his justification for doing nothing was sufficiently bizarre that I think you will be interested in this true story.

While attending a social event, I fell into conversation with an acquaintance I'll call Charlie. When Charlie mentioned that he was now retired, I asked him what he was doing with all his spare time.

He proudly responded by saying, "I do nothing. I sleep until ten in the morning. After breakfast, I shower, shave, get dressed, do a few things; and it's time for lunch." He sipped his wine and continued on, "After lunch I go to the club where I play cards and shoot pool with the guys for the rest of the afternoon. In the evening I watch television."

I listened in shocked silence as he supported his 'do-nothing' lifestyle with this next statement.

"Like I said, I do nothing and there's nothing wrong with that. When you read the paper, do you ever see a headline that says somebody died from doing nothing? Of course not, nobody dies from doing nothing!"

What an intriguing revelation. What he said was true; I have never seen such a headline. Most inactive people offer up excuses for their inactivity and make empty promises to change their ways, but not Charlie.

Charlie spoke of his 'do-nothing' lifestyle with the confidence of someone who had just found the secret to longevity. I suspect that he and his buddies at the club held similar views, and may be typical of many more that live a sedentary lifestyle.

Unfortunately, when Charlie's friends read his obituary, the cause of his demise will not read, "Died from doing nothing". His cause of death will be disguised by medical terminology suggestive of something more complex and most will never realize the connection to Charlie's sedentary lifestyle.

Charlie was unaware that he had been losing muscle tissue and gaining fat for many years. Now in his mid-sixty's and sporting a sizeable bulge around his waist he was typical of 52 percent of men his age; quite satisfied with his sedentary lifestyle and the freedom that accompanied his retirement. It never occurred to him that his inactivity and unhealthy eating habits were inviting a range of illnesses previously mentioned.

Sure, aging slows you down, but you don't have to throw in the towel when you hit 50, 60 or even 80. What you need to do is set new priorities and begin a new lifestyle. Your retirement could span two of three decades so don't waste it.

A few years after my encounter with Charlie, I learned that he did in fact die; but I never learned of the apparent cause of his death. As Charlie predicted, I'll bet it was not – from doing nothing.

You Can Control Your Health

Most of us have always believed that our genes will determine whether or not we become the target of chronic illnesses such as heart disease, obesity, diabetes, and cancer. As it turns out, researchers in the new field of 'epigenetics' have shown that genes are not as fixed as we thought.

Writing in the Huffington Post, on 05/16/11, Dr. Frank Lipman states:

"While each of us inherits our own unique, hardwired, unchangeable version of the genetic code, epigenetic factors such as lifestyle and diet can radically change what our genes do."

He then adds. *"Which means, you have a lot more control over your health than you think"*

Later in his article Dr. Lipman says, *"Most of our genes are actually modifiable and can be turned on or off. In fact, you are changing your genetics daily and perhaps even hourly from the foods you eat, the air you breathe and even the thoughts you think."*

He also advises that while some genes such as hair and eye colour are unchangeable, these unmodifiable genes represent only about 2% of our genetic makeup. Dr. Lipman is an internationally recognized expert in the field of Integrative Medicine. (Dr. Lipman granted permission to use the above quotes)

It Runs In the Family

The idea that our lifestyle choices can influence how our genes behave brings to mind the following incident that occurred several years ago while my wife and I were vacationing with another couple in Europe.

For some reason we were discussing how to stay healthy. Andy had a fairly large unhealthy waist size but I had never commented on it for fear of hurting his feelings.

Canoeing with the Club

Since we were talking about health, I decided to risk it and mentioned that he was carrying a lot of weight around his stomach. Andy seemed to take no offence as he responded by saying, "Yes I know it looks that way, but I'm built just like my dad, it's something that runs in the family."

I did not pursue the subject because it was obvious that Andy was unaware that his waist size created a health risk. A couple weeks after we arrived home Andy phoned me to say that he had just visited his family doctor and learned that he had Type 2 diabetes. His doctor told him that he had to lose weight. Andy took the doctor's advice to heart and began a regular walking program. Within a few months he lost his excess weight, looked better than ever and ten years younger. Andy is proof positive that having a body 'just like dads' is not necessarily predetermined by a gene; you are in control of your waist size.

Stay Motivated

Why are we not more active? Why don't we exercise when we know it's necessary for good health? We are inundated with information about health and healthy living through every form of media including newspapers, radio, television, and the net.

We should be well aware that our body needs exercise, but half the men and nearly sixty percent of the women in the 65+ age group remain inactive. Why?

In a National Population Health Survey more than half (55%) of Canadians stated they should do something about their health.

That is, they felt they should become more physically active, quit smoking, lose weight or improve their eating habits. Almost half of those who stated they should be more physically active also said there was something stopping them from becoming more active. Their reasons were such things as lack of time, lack of willpower, fatigue, and so forth which we will discuss below.

The fundamental reason for not being active is not lack of information; it is lack of motivation.

For that reason, I will now provide you with over a dozen ways to keep motivated and overcome the obstacles that get in your way.

Motivation is that drive you feel within yourself to accomplish or achieve something you want.

There are times when we all temporarily lose that urge to achieve. It's easy to get lazy, miss a few days or weeks and eventually stop exercising altogether. The challenge is to remain committed to your exercise program for an extended period of time. The following 16 techniques will help you stick with it.

The Rule

First, you need to make it a rule that exercise comes first!

Lack of time

Since this book is aimed at those who are about to retire, or are already retired, lack of time should no longer be a barrier. If you are not working full time, but still cling to 'lack of time' as a reason for not being active, you may want to rethink your priorities; your lifestyle may be out of balance. By not going to work you suddenly gained several hours of free time every day. Out of that extra time, surely you can find 30 minutes, four days a week for your body. Remember, it's the only one you will ever have.

An Obligation to Yourself

If over the years you planned for your retirement by building up a pension and putting aside a few dollars to help you enjoy your later years, you have an obligation to yourself to keep active. If you don't, you are sabotaging your own retirement plans. Why bother with financial retirement planning if you don't have plans for a healthy body?

Keep a Record

Buy a small book, call it your 'activity book' and use it exclusively to record everything associated with your activities.

Pair Up

Associate with like minded active people. Find a buddy; you'll be able to keep each other moving when needed.

Mark your Calendar

Use a highlighter to mark up your calendar to indicate the time of the day and the days of the week allocated for your activity. As you mark your calendar, mentally tell yourself that these days are set aside for your exercise program; they are 'taken' and only an emergency will you allow you to deviate from your plan. If for some reason you miss a couple activity sessions, don't beat yourself up about it. Focus on getting back into your routine again, that's what's important.

Be Flexible

Despite the above comment, be flexible. If you would like to change the time of day or days of the week you workout, go ahead and do it. If you would like to switch from walking to cycling do that too. Your goal is to keep fit and have fun.

Announce Your Intentions

Tell your friends and family about your new found regular activities. It's normal to quietly think, "I'm not going to tell anyone in case I quit". That's a mistake. You are looking for ways to stay motivated, and telling others is one way to ensure that you will stick with your plan. Six months from now you can boast that you are still out there walking.

A Small Reward

The Bruce Trail hiking Association (Ontario) publishes a small book containing a series of detailed maps showing various sections of the Bruce Trail. The total length of the Bruce trail from Niagara to Tobermory is 894 km. Whenever I hiked a section of the trail I recognized my accomplishment by marking the hiked portion of the trail with a yellow highlighter, then I entered the date of the hike and the name of the leader. Most of us need these small rewards to keep going.

More Rewards

Give yourself a small reward every time you take part in an activity. Your reward can be something as simple as telling yourself you did well.

If you feel better about yourself, have more energy and feel more cheerful make a note of it in your special book. One instructor I know ends each group activity session by leading the group in a loud applause. When I first witnessed one of those outbursts of applause I wondered what was going on, but soon realized that everyone was saying, "Hey, we did well and we feel great."

Too Tired to Exercise

If you are tired of being tired, exercise may be exactly what you need. Once you start exercising you will have more energy – not less.

Yes that's a fact; test it yourself. Start small with a five to ten minute walk and gradually increase your time each day. Do it again tomorrow and again the next day and the first thing you know you will love your outings. Your outings will not only be enjoyable they will become part of your everyday routine.

Recognition

If you do something truly significant like pulling someone out of a blazing fire, you will probably get a plaque from the mayor at a public ceremony, but in the meantime, while waiting for the big event, devise your own methods of getting recognition.

Willpower

There will be times when you just don't feel like doing anything active. Be aware that we all get that same feeling from time to time. We accept the flimsiest excuse to justify staying home rather than go on a walk, a hike or a bike ride. Unless you are ill, don't give in to your feelings of apathy (or is it laziness?) too often. Muster up all the will power you can, then get out there and do what you know will make you feel great. Focus on the fact that exercise, or if you prefer - physical activity - will add to your vitality and quality of life.

Dreams Come True

When you are out there swimming, hiking, walking, biking or doing the sweat & stretch thing, working your muscles and breathing hard, remind yourself that you are only doing what you dreamed of doing a few months ago. You're chalking up health benefits and you'll keep coming back for more.

More perceived barriers

Here's a list of reasons often given for not exercising. If you spot a barrier that applies to you, get it resolved. Speak to someone about your concerns and fears because although they may be easily resolved, they may be real problems in your mind.

- Fear of the strange, unknown world of exercise.

- Don't know how to get started or who to contact.

- Don't have the confidence to start something new.

- Fear that physical activity may result in injury or pain.

- Don't have a partner.

- A feeling that physical activity won't do you any good.

- Unaware of how good you will feel after a workout.

- Don't have transportation.

- You think you won't like it.

Be Aware of Envy

You may be surprised to learn that some people who are closest to you, even family members, who profess their desire to help, may actually sabotage your efforts to make a change that will improve your health. Such incidents are not uncommon, so be prepared.

Here's a factual example.

When Julie retired she was overweight and aware of it, so she joined a fitness club and cut back on her food intake because she was determined to lose that excess weight. I happened to see her soon after she had met her weight loss objective and she looked absolutely fantastic. She was in high spirits and proud of what she had accomplished.

Around that time she visited her overweight, older sister whom she had not seen since the emergence of her new sleek self. Her sister, seething with envy, pounced on Julie with comments such as; what have you done to yourself? You're nothing but skin and bones. You look terrible!

It was devastating for Julie to hear those remarks from the sister she had always looked to for approval.

To have Julie parading around as the stunning well proportioned younger sister emphasized the older sister's extra weight. In an effort to regain her older sister's approval, love and support, Julie soon returned to her old habits and regained her weight; just what the older sister wanted.

What's Your Life Expectancy?

If you were a runner about to enter a track and field competition you would certainly want to know the distance of the race before you crouched, ready and waiting for the blast of the starter pistol. And so it is with your own life expectancy; wouldn't it be nice to have some inkling of how much longer you have on this earth? You will never know for sure, but the insurance actuaries can give you a pretty good prediction.

As mentioned previously, today's life expectancy for Canadian men is 78.8 years and 83.3 years for Canadian women. You know how long the average person will live but none of us are average so let us turn to a source that gets more personal. Life insurance actuaries study factors that have an impact on our lifespan. As a result, their longevity predictions are more accurate than most. I invite you to play the Longevity Game provided by Northwestern Mutual Life Insurance. Here's what to do if you have access to the Internet. Go to their web site at: www.northwesternmutual.com. From their 'Learning Centre' category click on 'Longevity Game' and proceed with the game. While playing the game, notice that the risk factors such as, Smoking, Diet, Exercise, Weight, and Stress determine whether you gain or lose years in your longevity calculation. Once you have arrived at Northwestern's estimate of how long you may live, please make a note of it for future reference.

Raw numbers about how long you have to live may be surprisingly positive or shockingly negative, but it puts emphasis on the need to establish important goals for your remaining years. Like it or not, you know that most of your birthdays have already happened. In the future there will be fewer, and each one will be more precious than the last. You may find it unpleasant to entertain thoughts about your own demise, but let us be realistic; dying is inevitable. Now with Northwestern's prediction in hand, you are in a better position to decide how you want to use that precious time; your remaining years.

On the Internet

There are numerous web sites that provide excellent information about exercise and fitness. Here are three sites you may wish to explore.

- Health Canada's site at: www.hc-sc.gc.ca

- Heart and Stroke Foundation of Canada: www.heartandstroke.com

- The National Library of Medicine in the U.S. has a first-rate site at www.medlineplus.gov which includes information on exercise and fitness.

Making Retirement Better

- What if anything would you like to be able to do six months from now that you cannot do now? Be as specific as possible.

- Having read this chapter, please state one or two specific things you intend to do to make your retirement better.

Chapter 5

Eat Right and Live Well

There is small danger of being starved in our land of plenty; but the danger of being stuffed is imminent.

Sarah Josepha Hale

Jeff Keeping is a six-foot-six, 290 pound, 30 year old who plays football for the Toronto Argonauts. In October of 2012, the Toronto Star ran a front page story on Jeff and his need to pack away 5,500 calories every day to stay in shape for his job. Jeff says his occupation requires speed and agility, but first and foremost it's about being big and strong. He says, *"You need to maintain your weight, and your size because you don't want to have less muscle than the guy across from you.*

I'm sure you have heard it said that your calorie input requirement is largely determined by your level of activity. So how does your calorie requirement compare to Jeff Keeping's? If you look at the Energy Requirement numbers a couple pages further on, you can select your age group and activity level for the answer. Note that a woman between the age of 51- 70 with a low level of activity requires only 1850 calories daily; that's about one third of what Jeff needs to maintain his ability to intimidate the guy across from him.

So how does Jeff continue to look good and feel great even though he loads up on 5500 calories every day? It's his level of physical activity; Jeff burns off his calories in the gym and on the football field with daily practice sessions and weekly games.

The Focus of this Chapter

- Calories

- Nutrients

- Canada food Guide

- Body Mass Index (BMI)

- Weight Control

What is a Calorie?

Not everyone has the same understanding of what a calorie is or what role it plays in the food we eat. A calorie is a unit of energy. Specifically a calorie is the energy it takes to raise the temperature of 1 gram of water 1 degree Celsius. Calories are provided by fat, carbohydrate, and protein, which we'll discuss later on. Almost every bite of food we eat gives us energy, and the amount of energy in food is measured in calories. Just as your automobile runs on gasoline, your body burns food to produce the energy we need to survive. In short, calories are a measurement tool, like inches or pounds. Calories measure the energy provided by the food we eat.

How Calories Behave

When you consume more calories than your body needs to function, your body uses what it needs and stores the remainder in places like your hips, thighs and waist. If you eat fewer calories than you need and your body will draw on those stored fuel reserves. Sounds simple enough. Numerous studies have shown that if you cut your calorie intake you will lose weight; add exercise to your daily routine and the weight will come off even faster. The secret to weight control is to burn off as many calories as you consume. That's about it.

Exercise More + Eat Less (calories) = Weight Loss

How many Calories (energy) do we Need?

Knowing how many calories are in a specific food item is of little value unless you know how many calories your body needs each day. The following data from Health Canada provides an average calorie requirement for men and women in three adult age groups and three levels of activity.

Males (Calorie requirement per day)

Age	Sedentary Level	Low Active Level	Active Level
31-50	2350	2600	2900
51-70	2150	2350	2650
71+	2000	2200	2500

Females (Calorie requirement per day)

Age	Sedentary Level	Low Active Level	Active Level
31-50	1800	2000	2250
51-70	1650	1850	2100
71+	1550	1750	2000

Your individual calorie requirement may be different. The requirement for energy varies between individuals due to factors such as genetics, body size, and body composition. (These numbers are not for women who are pregnant or breastfeeding.)

Here is a description of the three energy levels mentioned above.

- Sedentary: You spend most of your day in a sitting position. You do very little physical activity.

- Low Active: You do not do enough physical activity to benefit your health.

- Moderately Active: You meet Health Canada's physical activity recommendations of at least 30 minutes of moderate activity 4 days a week.

Calculate Your Individual Calorie Requirement

Here are three Internet sites where you may calculate your personal daily calorie requirements.

- The Mayo Clinic provides a Calorie Calculator on their website at: www.mayoclinic.com/health/calorie-calculator/NU00598

- Calculator.net provides dozens of calculators including one for calories. An interesting site at: www.calculator.net

- About.com also has a calorie counter at: www.walking.about.com

If you want to lose weight, try to stay below your calorie requirements or increase your level of activity. Make sure you eat nutritious meals but don't restrict your calories too much; eating too little or losing weight rapidly can be unhealthy and dangerous. Remember, calories are not your enemy; they give you the energy you need to live a healthy life.

How many calories in the food we eat?

I doubt that anyone wants to become a calorie counter, but in the beginning, as you try to get the hang of how many calories are in the various foods you eat, there appears to be no alternative. The purpose of course, is to learn how to match the calorie content of what you eat each day, with your known calorie requirement or limit.

Calorie content from various sources	
Item	Calories
Beer Michelob 12 FL. Oz.	95.6
2 large fried eggs	184.7
4 oz. Chicken breast	110
1-Bockwurst sausage	253.4

Kellogg's frosted mini-wheat's (1 cup)	173.4
1-McDonald's Hotcakes with syrup & butter	560
1-McDonald's Angus deluxe sandwich	780
1-Tim Horton's Sour Cream Glazed Doughnut	340
1-Tim Horton's Chocolate Chip Muffin	410

Some of the above numbers are shocking when compared to your recommended calorie allotment for a whole day. Nutrition Guides are now available at Tim Horton's, McDonald's and many other fast food outlets.

Where to Look for Calorie Content

Calorie content is normally shown on the food package under Nutrition Facts. There are numerous websites on the Internet that offer a calorie count for every food you are likely to encounter. For example, visit the Fit Watch site at - www.fitwatch.com and you will find calorie counts as well as numerous other nutrition facts and ideas.

Purchase a book that may be called 'calorie counter' where you can find calorie numbers for almost everything.

Go to Health Canada's website at - www.healthcanada.gc.ca., where you can order free of charge the Nutrient Value of Some Common Foods (NVSCF) booklet. It lists 19 nutrients for 1000 of the most commonly consumed foods in Canada.

Burning Off Calories

You may sometimes wonder how many hours you will need to spend on your bike or the hiking trail to burn off the excess calories you consumed at that celebration dinner. Here are some regular activities many people do and the corresponding number of calories burned per hour. You can find a more detailed listing on the net at Harvard Health Publications.

Note that the numbers shown in the chart below are based on a 150 pound person. Lighter people burn less; heavier people burn more.

Number of calories burned per hour.	
Bicycling	544
X - country skiing	510
Gardening	340
Hiking	408
Racquetball	476
Kayaking/canoeing	340
Swimming	544
Tennis	476

Nutrients in our Food

A while back we spoke about the energy we get from food and how it is measured in calories, but we have not discussed the nutrients in food. Food provides two groups of nutrients:

1. Macronutrients: protein, fat, carbohydrates, and water
2. Micronutrients: vitamins and minerals

Here's how these nutrients compare in terms of calories.

- 1 gram of protein contains 4 calories

- 1 gram of carbohydrates contains 4 calories

- 1 gram of fat contains 9 calories

What stands out here is that fat contains more than twice as many calories as either protein or carbohydrates.

Empty Calories

You guessed it, foods and drinks that are known as 'empty calories' are all those tasty things you love to munch on throughout the day or snack on between meals.

Sure, these foods are high in calories but they are low in vital nutrients, hence the name "empty calories", because they contain energy but little in the way of essential nutrients.

Your body needs a certain amount of vitamins and minerals each day. When you eat a lot of foods that are high in empty calories it may create a nutrient deficiency which can result in a wide range of problems. Unfortunately, these foods always taste good. Solid fats and added sugars are the culprits. Solid fats are solid at room temperature, like butter and beef fat. Solid fats are found naturally in some foods, but they are often added when foods are processed by food companies. Sugars and syrups are added when foods and drinks are processed.

Here is a sampling of foods that fall under the 'empty calorie' category:

- Cakes, cookies, pastries and donuts which contain solid fat and added sugar.
- Sodas, energy drinks and fruit drinks.
- Pizza, French fries, chips and other deep fried foods.
- Ice cream and candy.
- Beer and wine and all alcoholic beverages.

Canada's Food Guide

To get the full benefit of Canada's colourful Food Guide you may order one or more copies from Health Canada at 1-866-255-0709 or email: publications@hc-sc.gc.ca.

Canada's food guide separates the food we eat into the following 4 food groups.

1. Vegetables and Fruit

2. Grain Products

3. Milk and Alternatives

4. Meat and Alternatives

The Guide also speaks to the number of servings we should eat per day and the size of each serving. Calories are not mentioned as they are automatically controlled by the number of servings and serving sizes.

Following the Food Guide Servings will:

- Contribute to your overall health and vitality.

- Meet your needs for vitamins, minerals and other nutrients.

- Reduce your risk of obesity, type 2 diabetes, heart disease, certain types of cancer and osteoporosis.

The Four Groups

Group 1 - Vegetables and Fruit

Health Canada advises that both men and women should eat 7 servings (that's 3 ½ cups) of vegetables and fruit a day. They suggest one dark green vegetable such as - broccoli, romaine lettuce & spinach, and one orange vegetable each day, such as carrots, sweet potatoes and squash. This will give your body the mix of nutrients it needs.

Group 2 - Grain Products

Health Canada recommends that you make half your grain products whole grain every day. Eat a variety of whole grains such as barley, brown rice, wild rice and oats. Enjoy whole grain breads, oatmeal or whole wheat pasta.

Group 3 - Milk and Alternatives

Drink skim, 1% or 2% milk each day.

Group 4 - Meat and Alternatives

Eat meat alternatives such as beans and lentils often. Choose two servings of fish each week. Eat fish, such as char, herring, mackerel, salmon, sardines and trout. Select lean meat or alternatives with little or no added fat or salt.

Magic in the Nutrition Facts Table

Health Canada's website includes an excellent area devoted to helping consumers understand the Nutrition Facts Table. The easiest way to access their facts table is to enter the words, 'Health Canada Nutrition Facts Table' into the Google search bar, then click on the Nutrition Facts site when it appears among the choices.

They have a great interactive site. Just click on any one of the Nutrition Fact's in the chart, let's say Protein, and a full page of data and information about Protein will appear under several headings such as:

- What is protein?

- Where can you find protein?

- How can you make a healthier choice?

- Helpful hints at the grocery store, and more.

Once you have absorbed all that information, click back to the Nutrition Facts Table, select another nutrient and the magic happens all over again. You may also wish to print their information pages for future reference.

Eat Right Ontario

The Dieticians of Ontario operate the website, www.eatrightontario.ca. This site is one of the most comprehensive nutritional websites around so I hope you make it your go-to web location for all your nutritional information.

Some helpful topics to look for on their website are:

- Nutrition Labeling Videos

- Videos on Healthy Eating

- Getting Your Vitamins

- Sodium/Salt

- Alcohol

- Healthy Eating on a Budget

- Seniors' Nutrition

- Recipes

The Glycemic Index

Since diabetes is common among retired folks this is a relevant topic for the over 50 group. According to the Canadian Diabetes Association, at least 20% of elderly Caucasians have type 2 diabetes, and more than half of these folks are unaware they have the disease. They also state that other ethnic groups such as First Nations and East Asian populations have a much higher rate of diabetes.

The Canadian Diabetes Association describes the Glycemic Index (GI) as a scale that ranks carbohydrate-rich foods by how much they raise blood glucose levels compared to a standard food. The standard food is glucose or white bread.

Eat Right Ontario advises that the Glycemic index can help people with diabetes make healthy food choices. The index is one of the tools one can use to control blood glucose levels. The GI ranks foods that are mostly made of carbohydrates. This includes grain products, fruit, milk, starchy vegetables and legumes.

The GI ranks foods from a score of 0 to 100.

- Foods with an index of less than 55 are considered to be low GI foods (favourable)

- Foods with a ranking of 56 to 69 are medium (acceptable)

- Foods which score 70 or more are considered high GI (use sparingly)

You can find a Glycemic Index on various health related websites. Eat Right Ontario has a useful index on their website at www.eatrightontario.ca. Enter Glycemic Index in the search box and you will find what you want.

Health Benefits of lower GI Foods

Eat Right Ontario points out these benefits from favouring foods on the lower end of the GI scale.

- These foods raise blood glucose slowly, which can improve your blood glucose levels after a meal.

- They are often higher in fibre. High fibre foods help you feel full and are important if you're trying to lose or maintain your weight.

- They may improve blood cholesterol levels, which is important for preventing heart disease.

Processing and cooking techniques

- Processing: Juice has a higher GI than whole fruit, mashed potatoes have a higher GI than a baked potato, whole wheat bread has a higher GI than stone ground whole wheat.

- Cooking technique has an effect on the GI rating. For example, al dente pasta has a lower GI than soft cooked pasta. Steel-cut oats has a lower GI than instant oats.

Note: Steel-cut oats receive less processing than traditional rolled oats. That means that it takes longer for your body to convert the starch in steel-cut oats to sugar. Thus steel-cut oats rank lower on the glycemic index.

How to prevent type 2 Diabetes

Health Canada's website lists 5 ways to avoid Type 2 Diabetes. I find it fascinating to discover that their five steps are almost identical to the health and fitness recommendations made to all retirees in earlier pages of this book.

Here's what they recommend:

- Maintain a healthy weight

- Eat a healthy, balanced diet

- Ensure regular physical activity

- Don't smoke

- Keep your health in check

Body Mass Index (BMI)

Today, the Body Mass Index is accepted worldwide as an easy to use reliable tool for identifying where you stand in four weight classifications. All men and women in retirement should be aware of the Body Mass Index and know which weight classification they fit into.

The World Health Organization began using BMI to define obesity in the 1980's. About that time Body Mass Index became the international standard for weight classification. Canada began using the Body Mass Index for weight guidelines in 1988.

The public first learned about BMI in the late 1990s, when the government began promoting healthy eating and exercise. The BMI has an impressive history and reports indicate that BMI is accurate, reliable and easy to use. All you need is:

- A scale to determine your weight

- A tape to measure your height

- A chart to determine your BMI

BMI is a number which reflects the ratio of your height to weight to estimate how much body fat you have. Too much body fat is a problem that can lead to a variety of health problems. Body Mass Index will determine which of the following weight categories you are in.

Weight categories	Body Mass Index
Underweight	less than 18.5
Normal weight	18.5 to 24.9
Overweight	25 to 29.9

Obese	30 and over

The easiest way to calculate your BMI is to visit a website that will do the calculation for you. But first let's view an actual BMI chart so that you can visually see how most charts depict the input data and determine the results. The BMI chart below is from the Canadian Guidelines for Body Weight Classification for Adults and is reproduced with permission from the Minister of Health.

To determine your BMI number, locate the point on the chart where height and weight intersect. Read the number on the dashed line closest to this point. For example, if you weigh165 lbs and are 69 inches tall, you have a BMI of approximately 24, in the Normal Weight Category: see descriptions below.

BMI Categories

Underweight: less than a BMI of 18.5 suggests eating disorders and being undernourished.

Normal weight: BMI 18.5 to 24.9 indicates the ideal, healthy amount of body fat and a minimal risk of health problems.

Overweight: BMI 25 to 29.9 indicates a moderate risk of weight related health problems. While being overweight indicates some risk to health; research suggests that regular physical activity and a nutritious diet can decrease many of the risks associated with being slightly overweight.

Obesity: BMI of 30 or greater is due to a high percentage of body fat. Extra body fat is associated with an increased risk of health problems such as diabetes, heart disease, high blood pressure, and some forms of cancer.

Anyone in this category should try to lose weight and make positive lifestyle changes. At least 2.8 million adults die each year as a result of being overweight or obese.

What's your BMI?

As you can see, it is easy to calculate your BMI. This is a good time to get an estimate of your own BMI. Remember that BMI numbers are guidelines, nothing more. If you practice a healthy lifestyle and you are generally in good health the chances are that you will keep your weight at a healthy level. Another way to determine your BMI is to visit one of the many websites that calculate your BMI once you enter your height and weight.

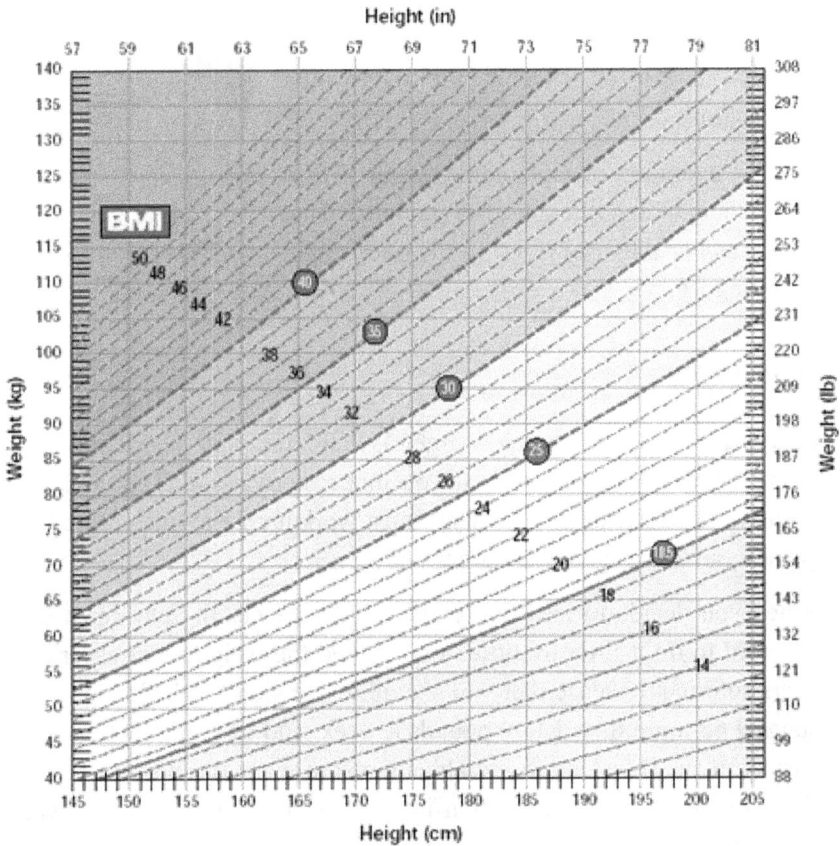

BMI calculator and App

You may wish to visit the US website of the National Heart, Lung and Blood Institute you will be able to calculate your BMI and download their BMI Calculator App for your iPhone.

Health of the Average Canadian

The Canadian Heart and Stroke Foundation have determined that:

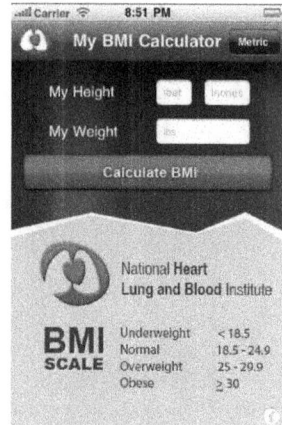

- The average Canadian adult male is 5' 9 in height and weighs 194 pounds. That gives him a BMI of 28.6 in the overweight category.

- The average Canadian adult female is 5' 4 in height and weighs 163 pounds. That gives her a BMI of 28.0 in the overweight category.

Weight Control

Carrying around too much weight is hard on your heart and blood vessels. When you gain weight you make more tissue. That additional tissue needs oxygen, so your heart must work harder to push more blood (which carries oxygen) to a larger body.

When you decide to lose that extra weight the health authorities stress the need to do it little by little. You gained the weight over a period of years so it makes sense that you should lose it slowly. Health specialists suggest no more than 1 to 2 pounds a week, and even that depends on a variety of factors. As you are already aware, your weight loss program should include a daily reduction in calories consumed plus an exercise program

A pound of fat equals 3500 calories. Therefore, if you reduce your calorie intake by 500 calories a day for a week you would theoretically lose one pound (7 x 500 = 3500). Most authorities suggest this is a sensible goal if you are trying to lose weight, keep in mind that it is easier to achieve your weight loss goal through a combination of increased activity and eating less. If your activity is walking, the easiest way to burn more calories is to walk farther. Gradually increase the amount of time you walk each day until you can walk for 30 to 60 minutes at a time most days of the week.

Canadian Adult Obesity at Historic High

According to a University of British Columbia study published Feb 27, 2013, obesity rates across Canada are reaching alarming levels and continue to climb.

Professor Carolyn Gotay the lead author in UBC's School of Population and Public Health says this:

"Our analysis shows that more Canadians are obese than ever before – on average, between one fourth and one third of Canadians are obese, depending on the region. Being obese or overweight significantly increases the risk of chronic illnesses, such as heart disease, diabetes, and some cancers,"

The Maritimes and the two Territories had the highest obesity rates with more than 30 per cent of the population estimated to be obese.

British Columbia rates were the lowest, but obesity still increased from less than 20 per cent to almost 25 per cent. Rates in Quebec remained below 24 per cent.

Eat Moderate Portions

Studies have shown that the average North American feels he or she is getting a real bargain if permitted to fill and refill a 12 inch dinner plate to the point of overflowing. Beginning in childhood we have been programmed to eat what's on our plate – "clean up your plate Johnny!".

Restaurant servings are getting bigger and bigger and most people flock to eateries that serve up huge portions. Apparently, restaurant rents and salary costs are the big ticket items, not the food. Getting more for your money is not good for your waistline or your health.

I have seen it suggested that when eating out, it's a good idea to pack-up what you perceive to be excess food before you begin to eat. Then when you have finished eating what you considered to be a reasonable amount of food, it's unlikely that you will resort to opening the take-home box.

Hara Hachi Bu - eat until 80% full.

In Okinawa, one of the Japanese islands, their traditional diet places emphasis on vegetables, whole grains, fruits, legumes and fish, with limited amounts of lean meats as a model for healthy eating and healthy aging.

They also control their calorie intake by following what is called 'hara Hachi bu', which means eat only until you are 80% full. Stopping at 80% capacity has been found to be a good strategy for avoiding obesity without going hungry. But the obvious question is, "How do you know when you're 80% full?" Since the stomach takes about 20 minutes to tell the body how full it is, we have usually stuffed ourselves before we get the signal to stop swallowing food.

The Okinawan's eat more slowly than we do, so their body has a chance to digest the food properly and get the fullness signal from their brain, before they have overeaten.

Apparently the Okinawan's Heart Disease rates are 80% lower than in the US. Their combination of diet and activity keeps their body fat low at a BMI between 18 and 22.

Sensible Suggestions

- Follow Canada's food guide for selection of nutritious foods as well as serving sizes.

- Place reasonably sized portions on your plate and you will feel quite satisfied when you have finished eating; if still hungry, you can always allow yourself a bit more.

- Serve meals already placed onto individual plates instead of placing serving bowls on the table. This will cause you to think twice before seeking a second helping.

- Eat a healthy snack such as a pear, orange, or apple between meals to keep from becoming overly hungry at meal time.

- Be sure you eat a nutritious breakfast every day.

- Skip dessert. It's an unnecessary add-on.

- Eat slowly and savour each bite.

- Follow the Okinawa 80% rule and you won't end up with that stuffed feeling at the end of a meal.

- We retiree's often end up on a cruise ship or an all inclusive resort where delicious food beckons at any time of the day or night. We have to muster up our self discipline and adhere to a self imposed rule which says, 'Stop eating - when you've had enough'.

- Don't eat a full meal after 8:00 in the evening.

- Always leave space between food items on your plate. You should be able to see the colour of your plate here and there, including an inch or so around the edges.

- You may have grown up with the understanding that you had to 'clean up your plate'. If you are overweight that rule no longer applies. Your health comes first.

- Dr. Arya Sharma of the Canadian Obesity Network and professor at the University of Alberta also says it takes roughly 20 minutes for the brain to sense fullness. Thus, if you gulp your food down, you won't get that fullness feeling until the damage is done. Pay close attention the next time you overeat and you will probably notice that it takes several minutes before you get that feeling that causes you to say, "Damn, I wish I hadn't eaten so much." By knowing about the 20 minute delay you can see why the experts encourage us to eat more slowly. Come to think of it, even my mother used to caution us to slow down. How did she know that?

Making Retirement Better

Now that you have a good idea of your personal calorie requirements, are familiar with the recommendations of the Canada Food Guide, are able to read a Nutrition Facts table, and know how to calculate your BMI, make a note of what changes you intend to make to your eating habits that will make your retirement better.

Chapter 6

Boost Your Income to Make Ends Meet

Money can't buy happiness, but it certainly is a stress reliever.

Besa Kosova

Money is one of those concerns which take on an importance of 10% if you have enough of it, but jumps to 90% in importance if you can't make ends meet. Whatever your income category, once you reach retirement you want to be able to enjoy your new found freedom, while feeling secure that your lifetime of savings are well protected by qualified and trustworthy people.

Finding a Consultant

It makes sense to seek out the assistance of a professional when it comes to your financial planning and investments. All of the major Banks as well as numerous financial institutions and individual financial consultants offer Retirement and Investment Planning. Most are a well qualified to attend to your needs associated with RRSP's, RRIF's, investments, mutual funds, estate planning and pension advice.

Choose your Financial Consultant with even greater care than your automobile mechanic. If you make the right choices you will work with and depend upon both for many years to come. A referral from a friend may be the best way to find a consultant you will be comfortable with. If that is not possible, use the yellow pages or the Internet to select at least three advisors, and then meet with each of them for a face to face interview. Note his or her qualifications; be satisfied that he or she can meet your needs and above all, be certain that you will feel comfortable working with that person.

You may not be as well versed in financial matters as you would like to be, but don't let that be an excuse for turning a deaf ear to the management of your personal finances. Once you engage a financial advisor to help you handle your affairs, you still have a responsibility to remain informed, ask questions and make the final decisions about what happens to your money.

Money is a key category that affects your life during retirement, and ranks up there with your health in importance. I have not included financial management in this book because several Canadian authors have already written excellent material on that topic. However, this chapter may fill an even greater need for those who are desperate to fill the gap between what they already earn and what they actually need to remain whole.

Why This Topic?

According to a survey by Sun Life Financial, released in February of 2013, 58 percent of Canadians expect to be working full or part time at age 66, while just 27 percent expect to be fully retired. The remainder are not sure. Other information indicates that about two-thirds of today's workforce does not have a registered pension plan.

In September of 2012, Don Lee writing for the Toronto Star stated that nearly 1 in 5 Americans ages 65 and older are working or looking for jobs – the highest in almost half a century. To put a happy-face on this information, research shows that many older Americans see working as a healthy way to stay active and productive.

Let's face it, some retiree's who do not have a defined benefit (DB) pension plan will have to resort to every trick in the book to maintain their current lifestyle as they grow older. Words such as 'frugal' and 'creative' may begin to take on a more prominent role in our everyday speech.

The purpose of this chapter is to give you some specific ideas of how to boost your income if you are having difficulty making ends meet. The process of reviewing these ideas may also kick-start your own creative brain cells to deliver up even more ideas on how to bring in more money.

27 Ways to Boost Your Income

- Disability Tax Credit
- Healthy Home Renovation Tax Credit
- You must apply for OAS
- Are You a Veteran?
- Working Longer
- Save on Auto Insurance
- Join CARP and Save
- Money Down the Drain
- Start Your Own Business
- Cut Costs – Two Cars to One
- Cut Costs - One Car to None
- Turn it Off
- Cash in on Seniors Discounts
- Curb Your Spending
- Smart Shopping
- Tidy Up
- Bartering
- Rent That Space
- Bookkeeping Service
- Make it and Sell It
- Teaching
- Writing
- Computer Specialist

- Mini Landscaping

- Be A Handyman

- Interior Window Cleaning

- Interior House Painter

Disability Tax Credit

You may not have heard of the Disability Tax Credit, yet the Bank of Montreal state that as of 2010, nearly 15% of Canadians were classified as persons with a disability. That means up to 5 million Canadians may be eligible for a number of benefits under Canada's Income Tax Act.

The Disability Tax Credit is a non-refundable tax credit that reduces the amount of tax a person will pay. This applies to those with a mental or physical impairment that meets the eligibility criteria.

If you qualify, it is possible to get $1,500 in tax credits in one year, and in some cases receive retroactive payments. If you think you may qualify for the Disability Tax Credit, you should meet with your accountant or financial advisor to discuss the possibility of applying for the Credit. If it appears appropriate to proceed you must:

- Complete the Government form T2201 which you can download from their website at: www.cra-arc.gc.ca/E/pbg/tf/t2201.

- Have your doctor complete the form.

- Send the form to the Canada Revenue Agency (CRA) where it will be reviewed to ensure that you meet the criteria.

Healthy Homes Renovation Tax Credit

If you are a senior 65 years of age or older, you may qualify for Ontario's new tax credit designed to encourage seniors to make their homes safer and more accessible. This tax credit applies only to Ontario, although other provinces may have similar programs.

The Healthy Homes Renovation Tax Credit is a permanent, refundable personal income tax credit for seniors and family members who live with them. If you qualify, you can claim up to $10,000 worth of eligible home improvements on your tax return. The amount of money you get back for these expenses is calculated as 15 per cent of the eligible expenses you claim. For example, if you spend and then claim $10,000 worth of eligible expenses, you could get $1,500 back.

Here are just a few examples of eligible expenses:

- Grab bars and related reinforcements around the toilet, tub and shower

- Handrails in corridors

- Wheelchair ramps, stair/wheelchair lifts and elevators

- Walk-in bathtubs

- Wheel-in showers

- Comfort height toilets

- Nonslip flooring in the bathroom

- A handheld shower on an adjustable rod or high-low mounting brackets

- Automatic garage door openers

To get the credit you must claim your total expenses on your personal income tax return. To do this, you will have to complete Schedule ON (S12). For more information go to the website at www.ontario.ca/taxes-and-benefits/healthy-homes-renovation-tax-credit.

You Must Apply for OAS

Here's something that some folks are not aware of. You will not automatically receive Old Age Security (OAS) benefits from Human Resources Development Canada. You must apply for OAS benefits, as well as for the federal supplement and the spouse's allowance.

Are You a Veteran?

If you are a Veteran, and have not signed up for the Veterans Program (known as VIP) through Veterans Affairs Canada, you may be missing out on a number of valuable services and benefits they offer. Don't wait; get more information by visiting their website at www.vac-acc.gc.ca. I am a veteran of the Second World War – 1st Canadian Parachute Battalion - and participate in the VIP program. They offer a valuable service.

Jim: 1942-45

Did you know that Via Rail usually offers veterans a 50% discount on rail travel? Next time you plan on taking a trip you may want to travel by Via Rail because the price is right for veterans.

Working Longer

Many seniors plan to keep working after 65. A 2012 study by the CIBC states that over half a million Canadians were involved in a start-up business, and the fastest growing segment was the 50 and over age group.

According to another survey, 6 out of 10 Canadians nearing retirement, plan to work longer so they can retain their benefits such as health and dental. If you are an older job hunter, here are a few websites that may be able to help you in your search.

- Top Employers for Canadians over 40. Check out this website at: www.canadastop100.com/older_workers.

- This organization is looking for younger seniors to provide help to older seniors in need: www.seniors4seniors.ca.

- Here is an employment website called 'Retired Worker' for 50+ Canadian job-seekers. They even begin by giving you 7 easy steps to posting your job search. Their website is www.retiredworker.ca.

- This site, 'Seniors for Jobs' is a place where job seekers post their resumes and employers post ads for available jobs. In essence it connects talented job seekers with Canadian employers. Find it at: www.seniorsforjobs.com.

- At this Government of Ontario website, you will find such articles as: Changing jobs at 45, a guide to midlife career moves, Resources for older workers, Work after retirement, and Embracing learning. - www.seniorsinfo.ca/en/azindex/J/Jobs.

Save on Auto Insurance

If you don't use your car during certain months of the year you can arrange to cancel your regular insurance and retain only the Comprehensive coverage (i.e. Fire, theft and vandalism) and thus save yourself significant money. The cancelation period must be for a minimum of 45 days.

Join CARP and Save

The Canadian Association of Retired People (CARP) offers a wide range of benefits to their members. Membership is quite reasonable at $20.00 per year, and is available to those who are 45 + years of age. We have been members of CARP for many years. They provide special prices in the following areas:

Auto and Home Insurance, Travel, Health Services, Automotive Roadside Assistance, Financial Services, Home Care, Funerals & Memorials, and more.

Visit their website at www.CARP.ca

Their Auto & Home Insurance is currently provided through the McLennan Group. We have purchased our Home and Automobile insurance through CARP for many years and have always been extremely satisfied with their service and their pricing. I do a comparison price check with other insurance companies every couple of years and have never found any reason to go elsewhere. CARP always has the best price. If you would like to save money on your Automobile

Insurance, I suggest you investigate what CARP has to offer. A similar organization, AARP exists in the US.

Money down the Drain

I know more than one person who pours hard-earned cash straight down the drain like clockwork every month.

You may say, "How do they do that"? Well, it is easy to do. Here are some examples.

- If you make monthly car payments to one of the Automobile companies and you are consistently late with your payments, you will be charged a penalty. Let's say it's $20.00 each month, that's $240.00 a year. *That qualifies as money down the drain!*

- If you are one of the 40% of Canadians who do not pay off your credit card in full every month you run the risk of being caught up in the credit card jungle of interest rate charges of 20% or more. Here are some simple rules to follow:

  - If you can't afford to pay for it when your bill arrives, don't buy it.
  - Pay your credit card in full on the day it arrives or you may forget.
  - Better yet, arrange for automatic withdrawal from the bank so that your credit card will always be paid on time and you have nothing to worry about.
  - *Interest paid on your credit card qualifies as money down the drain.*

- If you constantly get parking tickets for illegal parking, or for parking longer than your deposit allows, that's carelessness and *qualifies as money down the drain!*

- In this age of technology, there is never a good reason for paying a late fee. Pay your taxes, insurance, condo fees, and all other fixed payments by automatic withdrawal. You will never have to worry about missing a payment again.

Start Your Own Business

If you are looking for a way to boost your income by starting your own business, concentrate on something you are already good at. Chances are you will be more successful in a business where you use the skills you already possess.

By doing so you will provide a better product or service and you are more likely to enjoy what you do. Remember, you don't need to generate a lot of money in your business, just enough to cover the gap in your retirement income.

Here are a few basics that go hand in hand with starting a business, however small it may be.

- Find out if there is a market for the product or service you are considering.

- From your market research, establish an appropriate price for your product or service. If necessary get help with this, for if you underprice you will go broke, it you overprice you will have no customers.

- Clarify in your own mind exactly how your product or service will be different or better than your competition.

- Decide how you are going to attract customers and market your product or service.

- It is an absolute must that you maintain a proper set of books. If you do not have the time or know how, get help.

Cut Costs: Two Cars to One

We have always been a two car family. Even in retirement when the odometer on each car seldom registered more than 10,000 kilometres, we never wavered. Suddenly one day, the reality of our car situation hit home when a friend, glancing at our cars, commented, 'what a waste'. That got my attention; we were squandering our money. Within a couple of months we were down to one vehicle and it's working out just fine. We each enter our appointments in a small calendar, and then a quick glance tells us whether the family car is available or already spoken for. If we both happen to need the car at the same time, it's easy for one of us to rearrange an appointment. As a point of interest, in 2009 the Canadian average was 1.47 vehicles per household, so with one car we are not alone.

By disposing of one car we saved 100% of the fixed operating costs of that car, and $600.00 per year in parking fees.

Go to the Canadian Automobile Association's (CAA) website at www.caa.ca, for driving costs of various vehicles. Their charts for various vehicles show variable operating costs and fixed operating costs based on the kilometres driven. These costs are also calculated in terms of cost per kilometre.

Cut Costs - One Car to None

Matilda lives in a beautiful retirement condominium in the city of Mississauga. I met with Matilda, a very busy lady, to get her views on retirement, and as it turned out she alerted me to a method of saving money on transportation that had never crossed my mind. Midway through our conversation she said, "I sold my car and rented out my parking space". Knowing that she was always on the go, I asked her what she did for transportation without a car. She then told me that she had joined AutoShare, one of the new ways of getting around the city or anywhere else you want to go. She briefly explained AutoShare pricing and how much money she expected to save with her new approach to transportation. Everything seemed to fall into place; she drove less than 10,000 kilometres per year, there is an AutoShare pick up location nearby and she will collect rental income from her parking space.

Car sharing is perfect for anyone in Matilda's situation, or anyone looking for an alternative to owning a car.

Car sharing is now available in most large and mid-sized cities across Canada, the U.S., and Europe. With car sharing you become a member of a car share company and rent a car on an as-need basis. You pay only for the time and mileage you drive. The car share operator provides the gasoline, insurance, vehicle maintenance and parking.

There are three operators in Toronto with approximately 1,000 cars located across the city.

- AutoShare

- Car2Go

- ZipCar

If you are looking for a way to reduce your automobile costs, car sharing may be right for you. Check out their websites in your city, talk to someone you know who presently uses the car share system, analyse the numbers and decide what's best for you.

Cash in on Seniors Discounts

Here are the names of some of the Canadian establishments that offer discounts to seniors. Since the dates and amount of discount changes periodically, I leave it to you to determine the exact day and the amount of the discount. As always, it is up to you to ask for the seniors' discount, which is often quite significant. Some places offer the discount at 55 years of age while others insist on 65. Take advantage of their discounts, they are there for the asking; so ask.

Pharmacies

- Rexall Drugs

- Shoppers Drug Mart- discount on a certain day of the month.

- Pharmaplus – discount on a certain day of the month.

- Lawton Drugs - discount on a certain day of the month.

Stores

- The Bay - discount on a certain day of the month.

Other

- Bulk Barn and M & M Meats.

- Some beauty salons, health and fitness studios, offer a senior discount.

- OHIP covers yearly eye examinations for seniors 65+ performed by an optometrist.

- Most hotels offer discounts for either CARP membership or being a senior.

- Mandarin Chinese Buffet.

- McDonalds – always have a discount on senior's coffee.

- Most chartered banks offer discounts or eliminate certain charges for seniors, but this consideration appears to be on the way out.

- Movie theatres offer discounts to seniors

Transportation

- Greyhound Bus – Offer a discount of 10% for seniors on all tickets.

- Via Rail – Seniors discount depends upon availability.

- Public Transit - With appropriate passes, 65 year olds may ride the Metro or use public transit at reduced rates.

A penny saved is a penny earned

My mother had a proverb for every situation. She often reminded us - a penny saved is a penny earned - and we took it to heart. People have talked about pennies for centuries, but sadly, pennies are a thing of the past in Canada.

Apparently, this proverb was first recorded in George Herbert's Outlandish Proverbs, in the 17th century. The message being:

"It is as useful to save money that you already have as it is to earn more, or by declining to spend a penny and to save one's money instead, you are a penny up rather than a penny down."

Turn it off

Whether you live in a house or a condo get into the habit of being energy conscious. Don't waste electricity; it hurts your wallet and the environment.

- Turn off lights in rooms that are not in use.

- Turn off electric baseboard heaters during the summer months.

- Shut down your computer at night when not in use.

- Lower the heat at night, you will sleep better.

- Don't heat unused rooms.

- Don't waste energy by doing partial loads of dishes or laundry.

Curb Your Spending

Over the years we all get into the habit of spending money on things we don't really need. Now that you are retired and living on a fixed income, it's time to take a fresh look at some of the things you have been doing out of habit. Some of these may apply to you.

Living on a tight budget doesn't mean you can't have a good life, but you do need to get your priorities straight.

- Eat out less often. In any case a home cooked meal will be more nutritious.

- When you do eat out find a family restaurant that offers good value.

- If you are a smoker read the Don't Smoke chapter in this book. Maybe you will choose to kick the habit; at about ten bucks a pack, smoking must almost match the cost of groceries.

- Stop buying lottery tickets, another costly habit. How many people do you know personally who have won the lottery?

- Cut back on the number, frequency, and size or your alcoholic drinks.

- Be careful or you may end up spending a fortune in coffee shops. Stop it, or cut back.

Smart Shopping

- Always make a list of what you need before going off to shop, that way you will be more likely to keep your purchases to what you actually need rather than giving in to impulse buying.

- Keep your trips to the grocery store to a minimum. Fewer trips will also cut down on your car expenses and trips to the gas station for fill ups.

- Don't shop for groceries when you are hungry. You will buy less when you shop on a full stomach.

- Check grocery store flyers for what's on sale.

Tidy Up

As part of taking a fresh look at your new lifestyle, get rid of all that stuff you no longer have any use for. Check out your garage, storage room, attic, and closets. If you find clothing you haven't used for the past few years take it to Goodwill or the Salvation Army, where a needy person will make good use of what you no longer need. This may not put money in your pocket but it will help someone else and make you feel better.

Bartering

When I was a kid the rage was Big Little Books, which were in essence comic books about four inches square and a couple inches thick. I was constantly on the hunt for kids who had books to trade. If Billy had one that I wanted and I had one that he was looking for, we made a trade. Somehow we instinctively knew that trading books was a good idea because we gained access to the books we wanted to read, without spending cash (I'm talking nickels and dimes here); which was always in short supply.

People have been trading things forever and we still do; only now we use pieces of paper called money because it's more convenient.

Let's say you are an accountant who prepares Income Tax for folks in your community. Let's also assume that Harvey, one of your clients, builds patios and decks, and you are in need of a new deck for your backyard. It would make perfect sense for you and Harvey to arrange an exchange of services. Harvey builds your deck while you prepare his income tax for a few years.

No money changes hands but each of you acquires what you want. Be aware that the tax man may be watching, and there are guidelines to follow which you can look up.

There are numerous exchange opportunities like the one above which will save you money if you choose to barter.

Here are a three bartering websites that may interest you.

- BarterQuest at: www.barterquest.com is a cashless trading site. A trade occurs when a user makes an offer or counter offer, another user accepts the offer and the first user confirms the trade.

- Both visitors and members are able to browse trades on this website at - www.u-exchange.com/memberlist/Canada. You can search any Country or Canadian Province or you can be more precise by using their Keyword Search.

- HomeLink International is at - www.homelink.org/canada. They claim to be the world's original home exchange community. Their home exchange has been in business since the early 1950's.

Rent That Space

Every square foot of space has a value. If you own space that is not being put to good use, and you could do with a boost to your income, consider renting out that space.

- Rent out part of your basement area as a suite. Depending on your location and circumstances it may be a financially sound idea to renovate your basement in order to make it suitable as a rental unit.

- Rent a room. If you have an unused bedroom in your home you may wish to rent it out to a student or a single senior. You may want to go one step further and make it a bed and breakfast.

- Rent your parking space. If you live in a condo and own a parking space which you are not using, it makes perfect sense to rent it, for there is always a demand. If you live in a house, you may have driveway space that can be rented.

Bookkeeping Service

If you were a bookkeeper at some time during your working career and are familiar with the current bookkeeping software, this is a service that numerous small business owners always have a need for.

One way to get started is to contact accountants in your area who prepare income tax for small business owners. They may be able to put you in contact with folks who need your bookkeeping expertise.

Make It and Sell It

I always admire people who have the skill to turn a ball of yarn into a sweater or a plain canvas into a painting. If you happen to have a similar talent, there may come a time when you would like to exchange what you have created for some much needed cash.

Here's a website that will help you do that online. Go to www.etsy.com, where you can sell every type of craft imaginable. There is no membership fee; and it only costs a few cents to list an item. As you sell your product, Etsy collects a small fee on the sale price.

At the Etsy site you can view the myriad of items they bring to the market place. Here's a sampling of the type of crafts you can sell.

- Basketry

- Beading

- Candle's from Candles Making

- Handmade Jewellery

- Homemade candies

- Homemade soap

- Knitted materials

- Paintings

- Soft toys

If you have the time you may prefer to rent a table or a booth at a flea market or a farmers market and sell your product that way. You can also sell on EBay.

Teaching

Most good teachers love their profession and you may be one of them. There is great satisfaction in knowing that through your efforts, someone else will be able to acquire new knowledge or an additional skill. Not everyone is capable of doing that.

If you can teach people how to play a musical instrument, speak English as a second language, or act as a tutor in your favorite subject, there are thousands out there anxious to learn from what you have to offer.

Your purpose of course is to supplement your income. Take a look at these websites.

- At Udemy you can develop your own course and teach through their website. Here is their website: www.udemy.com.

- You may prefer to register as an online tutor with My Tutor World. They provide private online tutoring for learners spanning a wide range of subjects including Math, Sciences, and English. Their website is at - www.mytutorworld.com.

- Check out your local Community College. They may have an opening for someone with your particular talents.

Writing

If you enjoy writing here are a few suggestions you may be interested in.

- Explore the Elance website at www.elance.com. Elance is one of the better known places for writers and buyers to get together.

- Write the history of your hometown and other towns that appeal to you because of their historical significance. You can then market your book locally, where it will probably be a big hit, especially if you highlight the names of the original settlers.

- As a business, write the history of old homes in your city. That's what Robin Burgoyne has done since she began her business in 2008. It sounds like interesting work. While researching the history of an old house Robin has to dig into old files at the Land Registry Office, the City Archives, and the Reference Library. Visit Robin's website at, www.housestories.ca, where you can learn more about what she does, her pricing, and how she assembles her material for presentation to a client.

- There's a lot of job hunting going on these days within the 40 and older age group. Focus on this age category and help them write their resumes. They will appreciate your assistance and it will put a few dollars in your pocket.

Be a Computer Specialist

Almost every Canadian owns a computer. To be more precise, 96% of Canadian households have a computer and every one of them needs help to keep the dang things working.

If you consider yourself a computer guru there's a ton of work out there. All you have to do is decide what type of computer work you want to focus on and let people know you are open for business. Since you are probably a senior it may be appropriate to turn your spotlight on the over 50 age group as your potential customers.

Here's a sampling of the computer assistance we seniors need from time to time:

- Installing software programs.

- Learning how to use software programs such as MS Word

- Upgrading to a newer version of MS Word.

- Assistance with setup and operation of email.

- Ensuring that Backup is working.

- Arranging wireless connections.

- Fixing printer problems

- Resolving ongoing problems that always occur.

- Selecting and installing security systems.

- You may also want to consider web site design for small business.

Mini Landscaping

If you are a 'young senior', still able to able to lift, carry and dig without throwing your back out, mini-landscaping may be just the thing to boost your income. That's assuming of course that you have a green thumb. That's a catch all phrase that refers to people who know the difference between a daisy and a tulip, and know which plants need full sunshine and which ones prefer a shady spot. If you are green thumbed, you will also know how to trim a hedge, care for the lawn, weed the garden and clear away dead leaves.

I think of mini-landscapers as those folks who cater to the gardening needs of private home owners who either don't have the time or the inclination to look after their own lawn and garden.

If you have the knowledge, the skill and the good health needed to look after the gardening needs of the average homeowner, this could be an ideal job for a retiree looking for another source of income. In some cases it could be a perfect fit for a husband and wife team.

Here are some areas you will have to research and make decisions about:

- What area of town you will focus on.

- How to initially attract customers.

- What tools/equipment you will need.

- Pricing: by the hour or the job – and how much?

- Will you need another vehicle or will your existing vehicle suffice?

- How will you maintain appropriate bookkeeping and customer records?

Be A Handyman

A competent, trustworthy handyman is often hard to find. If you are a Jack of all trades and master of one or two, you should be able to meet the needs of numerous homeowners.

As a homeowner, I would expect a good handyman to be able to attend to normal door and window repairs, repair the steps and railing on my wooden deck, repair my roof, paint my shed, repair my fence, fix my leaky toilet, and do minor drywall work.

I would expect him to give me a quote ahead of time and complete the job in a reasonable length of time for the price quoted. I would also expect him to do good quality work.

That's what I would expect because I would have hired that handyman as a result of a recommendation from a friend or neighbour.

If you are a good handyman put an ad in the local paper, on Craigslist, in the local grocery stores, your church bulletin and other places you know about in your community. Good Luck.

Interior Window Cleaning

Now that condominiums clutter-up the landscape in your town and mine, there is a new business opportunity that has not been adequately filled. The condo corporation attends to getting your outside windows cleaned, but the unit owners are responsible for cleaning the inside. And in case you haven't noticed, most condos are surrounded by a lot of glass which calls for a yearly cleaning. A lot of condo owners are past the age of where they want to risk standing on a step ladder to clean their own windows while numerous others are too busy to take on the job.

That's where you come in, not to wield the squeegee, but to line up the business, organize the jobs, and hire young people to do the work. Specialize in the condo market; hire polite people who will respect the home owner's property, keep appointments, and do good work and I'll bet your business will prosper. I have seen it happen.

Interior House Painting

You may think that off duty firemen have cornered this market, but there's always room for one more. We have always hired Rick, a retired fireman, to do the painting in our condo. There are 3 reasons why we always call on Rick and recommend him to others;

- He does excellent work

- His price is right

- He is dependable

If you are a youngish retired person and looking for a way to keep fit while bringing in some extra cash, this may be the job you are looking for. By the way you better have the painting expertise to do good work. Rick always walks about to spec out what's needed, then provides a written quote, which includes the paint. He never exceeds his quotation, but he sometimes charges a bit less just to make his customers feel good.

Making Retirement Better

You have just read 27 ways to boost your income. If you have found one or more way to increase your income mark them well because they may go a long way towards making your retirement better.

Chapter 7

Change is Inevitable and Frequent

It is not the strongest of the species that survive, nor the most intelligent, but the one most responsive to change.

Charles Darwin

As you gradually move from one age bracket to the next, you will notice that you are unable to do many of the things that you could do with ease, just a few years before. We all encounter these annoyances because, as they say; it comes with the territory. It eventually happens to all of us, so don't be surprised when your turn comes along. You can't walk as far as you could last year, you can no longer climb that hill, squash is suddenly too strenuous, you can't stand the glare of oncoming headlights at night, you invariably forget where you left your car keys, you forget your grandson's name, you stumble for no apparent reason and you fall asleep two minutes after you begin reading your book.

The point is, how should we respond to these irritating failures in our ability to perform? Some folks close their fist and punch a hole in the wall, some curse and swear, while others complain to anyone within earshot.

Be smart: adjust, modify and compensate.

Don't fight what you can't control. If you find the headlights from oncoming cars are a discomfort when driving at night, there is no need to stop driving, just stop driving at night. Driving is a privilege you want to retain for as long as you can drive safely, so as you age, avoid major highways, stick to driving in your own neighbourhood, and trade in that 15 year old gas guzzler for a small compact car that is much easier to manoeuvre.

Exercise is a must, so if the hill is too steep, find a less undulating trail but continue your walking routine. If running has become too strenuous, switch to a more gentle sport like walking.

If you find yourself falling asleep when you want to be alert, take a nap after lunch to refresh your brain.

If family names are a problem, type them on a small piece of paper and sneak a peek at them just before the big hugs begin.

Whenever you feel age chipping away at your performance try to figure out a way to adjust, modify or compensate. As for stumbling, see your doctor.

If your health is okay, and you presently live in a single family home, a duplex or a townhouse with the freedom to walk out your door and step onto terra firma, stay put! Unless you have a handicap of some kind, don't rush into condo living - as I did - where you can't even putter about in your own backyard.

In a condo you won't have the pleasure of cutting your grass, working in the garden, cleaning out the eaves, parking outside, sweeping the driveway, tidying the garage, or waving to your neighbour across the street. So stay where you are for a few more years.

Active, Passive, and Frail

Retiree's are subjected to another type of change as they move along the age gamut from one year to the next. The change I refer to is not always connected to age; it is more directly related to our energy level, our level of mobility, our fitness level, and our mental agility. A number of people have ascribed a title to these levels of change but none appealed to me until I encountered the Royal Banks' description of – Active, Passive and Frail.

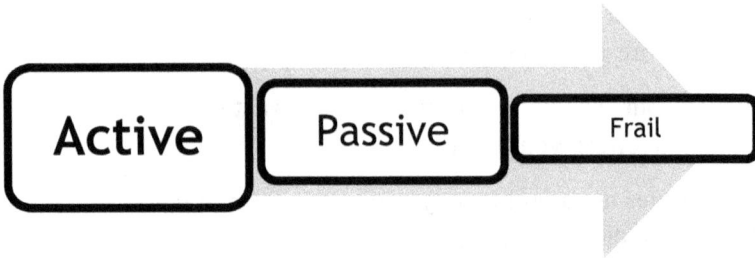

The RBC divides retirement into three appropriately named phases. Individual circumstances will dictate when you progress from one phase to the next, and as previously mentioned it may have very little to do with age.

Active – Generally you will be most active during your early years of retirement. Pack as much as you can into every day of your new found freedom during this period of your life.

This is the time to pursue the more strenuous activities on your bucket list, such as climbing Mount Kilimanjaro, visiting the pyramids, or exploring Machu Picchu. Engage in these more active pursuits while you are a young senior in your 'active' phase of retirement. If you postpone those more strenuous trips until you reach your passive or frail phase it will be too late. Not only will declining health and age hold you back; you will no longer have any interest in leaving the comfort of your own home. As you age your priorities also change.

Passive – This is the time when you get tired of rushing about; air travel, driving long distances, and staying up late begin to lose their appeal. Just the thought of racing to catch a connecting flight at London's Heathrow Airport is likely to bring on one of your headaches.

The most enjoyable part of your day may be that refreshing nap after lunch. Welcome to the passive phase of retirement.

Frail – This is the phase when many folks move to a Long Term Care facility where others will attend to your needs. Fortunately, there is a trend in Canada to encourage the elderly to remain in their own homes while the caregivers come to you.

Making a Change is Challenging

Thus far I have introduced you to the least difficult changes that will frequently occur as you age. If you can no longer climb that hill you adjust or modify your behaviour by walking on a more level terrain. That's a straightforward adjustment that you make without too much concern as you move through the aging changes of Active and Passive to Frail.

Managing change during your declining years is not always going to be that easy. Consider the following 3 situations:

1. For health reasons you know you should stop smoking but you don't.
2. For health reasons you know you should become more active but you don't.
3. For health reasons you know you should begin to eat right but you don't.

The reason you don't immediately stop smoking, become more active, or switch to a more nutritious diet is because it is usually extremely difficult to change the habit of a lifetime. When you reach retirement there will be times when making a positive change in your lifestyle will be a matter of life or death. If not that drastic it may be a choice between a quality lifestyle and a dreary existence.

If you understand what happens in your mind when faced with the need to change your lifestyle you are more likely to be successful at making that change for the better.

Stages of Change

The 'Stages of Change Model' was originally developed in the 1970's and 1980's by James Prochaska and Carlo DiClemente at the University of Rhode Island where they were studying ways to help smokers quit. Their change model has proven to be a useful tool in a variety of situations ranging from losing weight and getting fit, to alcohol abuse.

Their model shows that we tend to progress through different stages as we move toward a successful change; and we each move through the stages at our own pace. Thus, expecting someone to change a behaviour by simply telling him or her to 'begin a daily routine of 30 minute walks every morning", or "stop smoking", will accomplish nothing if that person is not yet ready to change.

Each person must decide on their own when it is time to move from one stage to the next. We are all different and each person needs to grapple with their own set of issues and their own timing as they move from one stage to the next.

Anyone entering retirement will soon learn that this is a period of their life when change is both inevitable and frequent. I refer to physical and mental changes that have an impact on your health and require some kind of action. Dealing with these issues is not a simple matter. It calls for a substantial commitment of time and effort, as well as mental strain. Being aware of what stage you are in as you proceed from one stage to another will help ease the transition as you change your behaviour, whatever it may be.

Here are the stages:

- Pre-contemplation: Refuses to acknowledge that a behaviour problem exists.

- Contemplation: Admits a problem exists but not convinced change is necessary.

- Preparation: Preparing to make a change.

- Action: In the process of changing behaviour.

- Maintenance: Actively maintaining the behaviour change.

- Relapse: When one falls back into old patterns of behaviour.

Stage One: Pre-contemplation

People in this stage don't want to make any change in their lifestyle and don't recognize that they have a problem. In their own mind they are convinced that their bad habit is not that serious. They minimize their problem and refuse to take any action to resolve their situation. With seniors, their lifestyle problems are often related to their need to lose weight, exercise, change their eating habits or stop smoking.

Thousands of people in this pre-contemplation stage are trapped in a state of denial, because they refuse to acknowledge the need to make a change in the way they live.

As I proceed through each stage of the change and describe the process I will simultaneously relate the true story of how a close friend, whom I will call Alex, as he progressed from Stage 1- Pre-contemplation to stage 5- Maintenance, where he is now actively maintaining his change in behaviour.

Alex in stage 1

About two years ago my friend Alex, in his early 60's, was seriously overweight. His weight problem would be a significant issue under normal circumstance, but in Alex's case, he had already suffered a heart attack so he was faced with that additional health concern. He was eating to excess, and did very little exercise. Although he had always been fairly active and maintained a normal weight, he seemed oblivious to the health hazard he carried around his waist.

It was both sad and frustrating to see his situation continue from one day to the next. Oh, how I wished he would progress to stage 2 – Contemplation.

Stage Two: Contemplation

When someone moves from Pre-contemplation to the Contemplation stage it follows that something must have triggered the change. It may have been something the person read, something he or she saw on TV, or a casual remark made by someone that prompted the person to move from one stage to the next. Determining what motivated the change is less important than knowing that the person has moved to the Contemplation Stage; that's what is significant.

In the Contemplation stage you are sitting on the fence, wondering what to do. You view your losses as being greater than what you would gain by making a change; you can't make up your mind. Just as you start to recognize the benefits of making a change, you also think about what you have to give up, to accomplish that change. Even if it is nothing more than giving up a dish of ice cream, a cigarette after a meal, or an extra hour of sleep in the morning, the thought of it emerges as more than you can accept.

Because of this uncertainty, the contemplation stage can last months or even years. The experts say that some people never make it past the contemplation phase. People will cling to the status quo, viewing any change as giving up something rather than gaining something. People in this stage never tire of constantly weighing the pros and cons.

In this stage you should ask yourself: Why do I want to make this change? What is preventing me from changing? Who may be able to help me make this change?

On the plus side, people in this stage are more open to receiving information, and more likely to accept help and reflect on their harmful habits. If you are an advisor or friend to someone in the contemplation stage, you can help by identifying the positive outcomes that change will bring about.

Alex in stage 2

Alex maintained his sedentary lifestyle, his negative attitude towards life and his unhealthy eating habits for a couple of years. Then one day while we were driving through a large wooded area near where he lived, he said, "There are a lot of good hiking trails around here, and I've been thinking it might be a good idea to come up here on the weekends to explore some of them."

I was ready to jump with joy for I realized he had moved out of Stage 1, Pre-contemplation, to stage 2, Contemplation. I tried not to display too much enthusiasm, but agreed that he was onto a great idea and encouraged him to get hiking maps of the area and make other preparations for his return to active living.

Alex added that he would have to purchase some good walking shoes or hiking boots, and that tended to confirm his intentions – he was getting ready for the next step. I was overjoyed.

Stage Three: Preparation

In this stage, you are committed to making a change. You will begin to gather information about what you need to do to change your behaviour. You may get out a pen and paper and begin listing all the things you must do; what your intentions are, what you must purchase, whom you need to contact.

For example, if your goal is to lose weight, you will get best results by starting an exercise program and reducing your calorie intake at the same time. You may also get involved in other positive steps such as joining a health club, or reading health related books and magazines.

Alex in stage 3

The next time I heard from Alex he told me he had purchased walking shoes and was walking every morning on paths in a wooded area near his home. He said he enjoyed it and looked forward to his walk before beginning his work day. This was a switch from wanting to explore hiking trails, but who cares; he has embarked upon a more active lifestyle.

Stage Four: Action

This is when you believe you can do it, and you are actively involved in dumping your old behaviour for the new. You start taking action toward accomplishing your goals. If you have in fact taken positive action, congratulate yourself and give yourself a small reward for taking these positive steps. Reinforcement and support are important here so revisit chapters of this book which are loaded with suggestions related to overcoming obstacles and how to stay motivated. Review your commitment to yourself and develop plans to deal with slip-ups, should they occur. People in this stage are open to receiving help and will seek support from others. This is the time to pat yourself on the back – reward yourself for your success.

111

Alex in stage 4

A lot of unexpected, exciting changes were happening in Alex's life. He's really turning his life around; all because he began taking a 30 minute morning walk.

For years Alex had been driving to a local restaurant for breakfast every morning where he loaded up on bacon, eggs, pancakes and other fattening foods. Alex told me that he had recently been questioning his motives for heading off to the eatery every morning and he concluded that the attraction was the morning newspaper.

As part of his turnaround he subscribed to the Toronto Globe and Mail and put a stop to his morning visits to the restaurant. Now, he's off on his morning walk first thing each morning. On his return he's energized and ready for a healthy breakfast at he reads the morning paper without leaving the breakfast table. Alex runs a successful business from his home.

Stage Five: Maintenance

If you have reached your goal you are in the maintenance stage. You are now consistently enjoying your new lifestyle, doing whatever you set out to do -   whether it's not smoking or eating right - you are in the maintenance stage. Now you have to avoid any temptation to return to your old lifestyle. This is a time when it pays to remind yourself of how much progress you have made and the success you have achieved.

As you progress through your own stages of change, it can be helpful to re-evaluate your progress as you moved through the stages. And remember: it is not unusual to have a relapse; to attain one stage only to fall back to a previous stage. This is just a normal part of making changes in your behaviour.

Alex in stage 5

The last time I spoke to Alex he revealed another positive outcome to his new lifestyle. He said, "Do you remember me telling you that – I wish I could stop thinking about work problems the last thing at night and the first thing in the morning"?

I told him that I remembered that conversation and recalled how much it bothered him. Then he said,

"That's all changed now, my last thoughts at night are about my morning walk, and when I awake in the morning the first thing that comes to mind is my walk, because I really enjoy it."

Alex's attitude towards life has also improved; he has lost weight and pulled his belt in a notch or two. It's truly amazing how one small change, like taking a 30 minute walk every morning, can eventually have a far reaching impact on your total lifestyle.

Relapse

When seniors have a relapse, it's usually associated with failing to follow through with an exercise program, failing to eat right, or some other health related goal. When you have a relapse, you might experience feelings of failure, disappointment, and frustration. The key here is not to let a setback undermine your self-confidence or make you feel that you have somehow failed. Relapses are a common occurrence and they happen to most of us at one time or another.

What you need to do is rethink why that goal was important in the first place; think back to what motivated you back then, and make plans to get started again. If you can determine what triggered the relapse you may be able to avoid letting it happen to you again.

Alex in stage 6

So far, Alex has not returned to his old habits, and based on his past history, it's my guess that he will continue with his new lifestyle into the foreseeable future.

It's a Great Feeling

Eventually you will reach the point where your bad habit is no longer a part of your lifestyle; getting that monkey off your back will give you a feeling of great satisfaction.

It may be that:

- You don't smoke anymore and have no fear of ever smoking again.

- You are back to your normal weight and you're confident you will remain that way.

- Exercise has become a way of life and you intend to keep it that way.

That's the kind of feeling that will give you true peace of mind. Now you can pat yourself on the back and say – 'I did good'.

Goal Setting for Change

Let's assume that you are in Stage 3 – Preparation, and anxious to get started on at least one behaviour that you would like to change.

Before forging ahead it's a good idea to think through exactly what it is you want to accomplish – i.e. your goal. Here I'll discuss an approach that will help you clarify your thoughts and help you stay on track once you get started.

As one wise man put it, if you don't know where you are going, any road will get you there. And yet many of us do not have specific goals to focus on and motivate us as we proceed through life. People often accept what comes their way, never stopping to think that they can in fact control their time and their life if they put their mind to it. That's because a lot of people are not sure what they want.

Goals make a difference no matter what your age. You may have heard of the kindergarten teacher who walked around her classroom observing each child's artwork. As she got to one little girl who was working diligently, she asked what the drawing was.

The girl replied, "I'm drawing God." The teacher paused and said, "But no one knows what God looks like." Without missing a beat, or looking up from her drawing the little girl replied, "They will in a minute!" That child knew exactly what she wanted to accomplish; a drawing of God, one minute from now. That was her goal statement; a clear, concise statement of an end result.

During the Stages of Change process, you finally recognize the need to replace an existing behaviour for something better in Stage 3, Preparation. Making a change to any aspect of our lifestyle is never an easy thing to do; it's usually easier to stick to our old way of doing things. Yet, you want to make the change because you know it's the right thing to do. There is a process that will help overcome our natural resistance to change and at the same time, enable us to embrace a new improved behaviour. That process is goal setting.

As a senior, the lifestyle improvements you will likely seek are those associated with finances, relationships, health, exercise, weight control, and self-improvement. While we often want to make changes in our life, we don't always know where to start. Goal setting will help identify exactly what you want to accomplish. An acceptable goal statement must meet these criteria.

- Be Specific

- Be Measurable

- Be Realistic

- Be Personal

Be Specific

When you write down a goal statement you create a contract with yourself and set in motion a process that helps you carry through. It is not absolutely necessary to write out your goals, but by doing so you clarify your thoughts and arrive at a more precise statement of what you want to accomplish. Your goal must be a clear, concise statement of an end result or desired outcome.

When preparing your goal statement, focus on the goal, not the Action Plan which tells you how to get there; that comes later. By its very nature, a goal is a statement of something you intend to accomplish in the future - that's your focus. Try to get a clear mental picture, visualize yourself after you have achieved your goal.

A statement like, "I am going to get into better shape next year", is of little value. It's no more than a vague comment about your intention, with nothing to indicate how you will know when you are 'in shape'.

Be clear about timing, and be precise about your intended outcome. A better goal statement would be, "Beginning next week, I will workout at the gym for 1 hour, twice a week for the next 6 months."

Be Measurable

A goal statement must include such things as dates, times and amounts so that your achievement or lack of it can be measured. If for instance, you write a goal statement about becoming more physically active, you must include a start date, and some way of determining when you have accomplished your goal.

Be Realistic

When writing a physical activity goal, take into account your present age and your health. If necessary, consult with your health care professional. Don't set your goals so high they are unattainable, for then you're sure to fail, and nothing is accomplished. Identify obstacles that may hinder your ability to reach your goal. If obstacles come to mind, figure out ways to overcome them.

Be Personal

Your goal must belong to you and state what you want to achieve for yourself, not someone else. Don't set too many goals and thus run the risk of accomplishing none of them. One goal aimed at improving your physical fitness is probably enough. Your brain needs time to get used to the idea of your new regular activity. Remember that slip-ups are normal; just be sure to get back on track.

These following goal statements are specific, measurable, realistic and personal.

- Ted- Beginning this week, I will work out at the gym for 1 hour, three times a week for the next 6 months.

- Julie - By (date), I will have lost 40 pounds and my Body Mass Index will have moved from overweight to the healthy weight category.

- Ken - Beginning (date), I will volunteer at the local food bank one evening per week for the next 12 months.

Note that the first and second statements focus on two different levels of activity. Ted is interested in maintaining his present level of fitness by working out three times a week. Julie identifies her goal by the end result; lose 40 pounds, which is just fine. Her action steps will define exactly what she intends to do to lose those 40 pounds. Each goal is designed to meet the specific needs of an individual, and both are acceptable.

Action Plan

Every goal statement needs to be followed by a plan of action in order to turn the goal into a reality. For example, Ted may convert his good intentions into feet on the treadmill by following an action plan something like this:

- Find out what gym facilities are in his neighbourhood.

- Examine the pros and cons of each gym by visiting two or three that appear to be the most promising.

- Select the most suitable gym.

- Meet with the appropriate person and decide upon a workout program.

- Purchase whatever gym attire is necessary.

- Ted should then enter all gym times and dates on his calendar as a reminder that these times are reserved for his workouts.

Making Retirement Better

You are aware of the need to adjust, modify and compensate as you move from one decade to the next during retirement. You know about the Stages you go through when making a behavioral change, you know how to set goals and prepare an Action Plan. Please make a note of the items in this chapter that you intend to act upon because it will make your retirement better.

Chapter 8

Don't Smoke; It's Worth the Effort

The cigarette does the smoking - you're just the sucker.

Author Unknown

In July of 1988 I sat across the desk from Dr. Chris Feindel, Cardiovascular Surgeon at the Toronto Western Hospital. He was discussing my open heart by-pass surgery (caused by smoking) which was scheduled for the next morning, when he said:

"Jim, here's what you have to do to stay healthy after the surgery."

I borrowed a sheet of paper from him to make a few notes of what he was about to say, for this was undoubtedly the most important event in my life and I wanted to remember every detail of his instructions.

Although Dr. Feindel is a soft-spoken man, his message came across loud and clear. He was about to save my life this time, but after surgery it would be my responsibility to do what was necessary to stay alive and well. I jotted down a few notes and saved them.

I recently retrieved those notes I made on that borrowed sheet of paper some twenty-five years ago and was surprised at the sheer brevity of what I wrote down. Here is what he said, just a few simple words with a powerful message:

- Exercise

- Eat Right

- Don't Smoke (I had been a heavy smoker for 40 years)

Since Dr. Feindel was talking about the essentials of my life, I expected to find more, but that was it! That was the extent of his advice. If heeded, the doctor's three warnings encompassed all that was necessary to promote a healthy lifestyle. Furthermore, his words of wisdom are as valid today as they were back then in 1988.

The surgery went well and like thousands of other heart by-pass patients I was up and around in record time. But I was still faced with the three major challenges: exercise, eat right, and don't smoke. I was at my 'fork in the road'; would I make the right choices?

Your Fork in the Road?

It sounds simple enough, all I had to do was quit smoking, start eating right and exercise, but talking about it and doing it are two different kettles of fish. I knew that I had to get those three monkeys off my back or I would be marking time, waiting to die for the remainder of a very dull life.

You may be in a similar position at age 50, 60, 70 or somewhere in between. You may be retired or about to retire when out of the blue something happens to make your life less beautiful than it was the day before. Maybe it will be a little thing, like having to move your belt out one more notch; or it may be a T.V. Commercial or a magazine article that makes you acutely aware that you were out of shape. Or, god forbid, you had to walk up a flight of stairs and found yourself totally exhausted.

Whatever your situation, you may be at your 'fork in the road' with your own monkeys to shake off. Whether you get a gentle warning about your health, or like me, get hit with a sledge hammer, it is essential that you do something about it.

My Three Monkey's

I'm pleased to let you know that I ditched all three of my monkeys.

Exercise. After my heart by-pass I followed Dr. Feindel's advice and made active living a way of life.

Eat Right. Thanks to my wife Olga, I now 'eat right' all the time. Eating Right is critical to good health, but having already devoured the EatRight chapter you already know that.

Don't Smoke. This was the toughest hurdle of all and I would like to tell you something about it. My first surprise was to learn that smoking was the cause of my heart problem; two of my arteries were almost clogged with cholesterol, and according to the doctors, that came about because of forty years of smoking. That was news to me, naivety I suppose, but in 1988 I had no idea that smoking could cause heart disease.

My battle with the cigarette

I cut back on my smoking a few weeks before my heart bypass surgery, but Dr. Fiendel's pep talk was the final clincher; I vowed to never take another puff – wilful thinking at its best.

At the time I had no idea how I was going to accomplish the challenge or how difficult it would be. After my surgery I enrolled in the Cardiac Rehab program offered by the hospital. Thus while attempting to get my body back into shape I was also struggling with my self-imposed stop smoking program.

Back then – before the Internet – there was almost no support for people who wanted to quit, you had to devise your own techniques, talk to others who had quit smoking and muster-up all the willpower you could to kick the habit. Seeking help from the outside, I responded to three sources in hopes that they would improve my ability to quit.

- I went to a doctor who offered help through hypnosis. I was smoking again within hours of being hypnotized, so that was unsuccessful.

- I signed up for a program that required attendance at three or four sessions. It proved to be an amateurish idea cooked up by someone wanting to make some easy money. A waste of my time and money.

- I attended a lecture given by a medical doctor. His presentation was very helpful and I put his strategies to good use.

Today, there are dozens of professionally developed stop smoking programs available at no charge, so your chances of being successful are much higher than they were 25 years ago. Nevertheless I did have one strategy which helped me throughout the prolonged struggle that lay ahead. I decided that my long term goal was – stop smoking – and I promised myself that despite slip-ups or relapses I would never give up on my long term goal, to stop smoking. That promise turned out to be critical to my ultimate success.

Despite our carefully thought out plans, fate often intervenes with hurdles that hamper our success. Six months after I began my stop smoking program my first wife was diagnosed with cancer. That news wrecked havoc with my ability to distance myself from nicotine fixes, so most of the gains I had made up to that time were lost. My wife died eighteen months after her cancer diagnoses.

During that difficult period my stop smoking plan was in total disarray, but I never lost sight of why I had to quit smoking; knowing that I had heart disease, my life was at stake. Eventually, after two years I was able to call myself a non-smoker. Keeping my ultimate goal front and centre enabled me to keep on trying and eventually I ended up on the winning side of my battle with the cigarette.

Parts of my plan that worked

I keep a record of my progress as I moved from smoking a full pack a day to becoming a non-smoker. Although my progress was all over the map I did at times, keep a record of the number of cigarettes smoked in my daily calendar. Thus I could quickly view my progress and feel good about it. It gave me a small reward and kept my spirits up.

This is a period when you should have several positive self talks every day. When you first hear about self-talk you may associate it with something that kids do, but on the contrary, positive and negative self-talk has a significant impact on our actions. If you engage in positive self-talk such as telling yourself that one day things will improve, that one day you will lose your craving for nicotine, that one day you will be a non smoker, that one day you will succeed, it will have a positive effect on your ability to achieve your goal, whatever it may be. I am a firm believer in positive self-talks and I made frequent use of the technique while trying to quit. I credit positive self-talks for much of my eventual success.

I created a non smoking environment in my home, which meant discarding everything that might remind me of smoking. I got rid of all ashtrays, discarded all lighters and all but one small pack of matches. When I could not resist the urge for a smoke, I went outside. I never smoked in my home or the car.

Finally one day I realized that the smoking monkey was no longer on my back, he was gone forever. It was a tremendous relief to be free from that habit. It wasn't easy but it was worth the struggle.

More recently I heard of a great idea for anyone trying to quit. Here it is; type out and carry around a list of all the reasons (incentives) you have to quit smoking. Include family reasons, health reasons, saving money and anything else that may apply to your situation. Whenever you are tempted to light up, get out that list and read it over. It will probably cause you to postpone that smoke.

How did I benefit?

As a heart disease survivor my main benefit was tied to my health. I was now able to walk, hike and canoe without being short of breath, I felt better than I had in years, I was full of energy and enthusiasm and I always had a project on the go. If I had not stopped smoking I would have been dead and buried many years ago. As it turned out I have lived a happy and rewarding life for 25 years since butting out.

While saving money was not a high priority for me, no one can scoff at saving $3,000.00 a year. That's roughly the price of cigarettes for one person for a year; make that $6,000.00 if you and your wife both smoke. My teeth are not the pearly whites you see on television, but they are no longer stained with that yellow tinge created by tobacco smoke. My breath no longer reeks of the stale smell of tobacco. Over the years, my clothes, our drapes, the furniture, and even the carpet have been replaced, and none of it gives off that nauseating smell of stale tobacco.

Now when I walk out the door all I have to remember is to slap a ball cap on my head and put the house keys in my pocket. If I was a smoker I would also have to ensure that I had an adequate supply of cigarettes because they were as important as fuel in the gas tank.

My smoking legacy

If you happen to be a smoker who is not yet convinced that quitting is worth the effort, add this to your catalogue of reasons for quitting sooner rather than later.

If you wait, like I did you may need open heart surgery, where the surgeons replace your clogged arteries with substitute veins or arteries from another part of your body. When that happens, your journey with heart disease has only just begun. From that day forward you'll be popping a mixture of several pills every day in an effort to keep your heart disease (Cholesterol etc.) under control. Despite your best efforts you will probably end up in the hospital every 5 to 10 years for insertion of one or more stents. Words like angina, angiogram, angioplasty and heart attack will become part of your new everyday vocabulary.

Whatever your age, if you quit now rather than later you can substitute the major problems associated with bypass surgery for a short period of discomfort as you wean yourself off nicotine.

Recollections of 4 Who Quit

It was easy for Katie

During a conversation with Katie who had smoked for 35 years, I asked her how difficult it was to quit. Without hesitation she said,

"It was easy, I had been thinking about it and planning to quit for so long that when I finally got around to quitting it was a relief to have it over and done with. I just quit and never looked back."

Not everyone is so fortunate, but every once in a while you may hear of similar experience.

Maria and her Grandson

Maria was excited about joining her son, daughter in-law and one year old grandson on a two-week trip to Italy. She looked forward to spending time with her only grandson, but there was a problem. Maria was a smoker; she had no intentions of smoking around the child and she hated the idea of constantly darting off for a quick smoke around the corner. There was only one solution - quit smoking. She thought about it; she considered the idea from every angle and weighed all the pros and cons. Would having time with her grandson be a strong enough attraction to outweigh her need for a cigarette every hour or so for the next couple of weeks?

Maria told me this was not her first kick at the can; she had tried to stop smoking several times before without success. She told me she went for long hikes as she pondered her dilemma and searched for the right answer.

Eventually everything became clear, she no longer had any doubts, and she knew she could conquer her habit. Her love for her grandson won out over the draw of the nicotine. Maria stopped smoking. She made the trip to Italy, had a great time and never smoked another cigarette, not ever.

Greg from Australia

Greg's quit smoking technique was so unusual and effective that it may cause a tsunami of smokers to seek out the same treatment. Greg spent most of his working career as a manager in the nightclub industry where he was constantly exposed to a thick layer of cigarette smoke. He was a smoker so one would think that second-hand smoke would have no effect, but apparently it did. Greg was constantly wheezing and so short of breath that he was concerned he may have emphysema. His wife wanted him to see a doctor, but Greg had another idea.

He knew that smoking was the culprit so he decided to quit. The question was – how was he going to stop doing something he had enjoyed for the past 30 years. Still living in Australia, he heard about a doctor who used acupuncture to treat people who wanted to give up smoking, so he located the doctor and made an appointment. The doctor told Greg to be at his clinic every morning for five days at 8:00 a.m., at which time he would insert 5 acupuncture needles to the outer flap of his right ear, and that would to be followed by a 30 minute quiet rest.

Greg told me that he stuck to the schedule and after his first two visits his urge to smoke was considerably diminished. By the time he had completed his fifth treatment he said he had absolutely no urge to smoke. Greg never smoked again and that was twelve years ago. I asked Greg what his greatest health benefit was from not smoking. He thought for a moment and then said "Well, I can breathe now."

Iris and the Virgin Mary

When Iris quit smoking it was a done on the spur of the moment. Over the years she had built up a heap of anger at how difficult it had become to light up and smoke a cigarette in peace. She couldn't smoke in her own home because her husband was allergic to cigarette smoke; she had to go outside and that annoyed her. She couldn't smoke on the bus and she couldn't smoke at work. The whole smoking thing irritated her, and she was angry at herself for being hooked on cigarettes for over 30 years, when she knew it was affecting her health.

At home Iris always kept her cigarettes and lighter on a table in the entry hallway. One day as she was about to leave for work she walked towards the table in the hallway, reached for her cigarettes and hesitated; then she grabbed the cigarette package, squeezed it as hard as she could and threw it into the garbage.

Then she said a Hail Mary and prayed to the Virgin Mary to give her the strength to quit smoking. As Iris told me this story she reached into her purse, took out a small picture of the Virgin Mary and showed it to me. She wanted to make sure that I knew exactly who her benefactor was. (Not wanting to diminish her enthusiasm, I did not mention my years as an altar boy or my Catholic background.) Iris then told me that while she was trying to quit, she prayed to the Virgin Mary every day for the strength to resist the temptation to smoke and it worked; she never smoked again.

Help is Available

If you want to stop smoking and need help to get started there are numerous organizations out there anxious to help. In the pages that follow I will direct you to websites of several locations where you can get free support. All you have to do is ask.

According to Health Canada's most recent information, 17% of the Canadian population aged 15 years and older are current smokers; that's about 4.7 million Canadians. They range from a low of 14% in British Columbia to a high of 21% in Saskatchewan, Nova Scotia and Manitoba.

You may find valuable assistance at the following websites.

- The Canadian Cancer Society website at www.cancer.ca

- Smokers' Helpline is a free, confidential service operated by the Canadian Cancer Society. They offer support and information for those who want to quit smoking. Their website is at - www.smokershelpline.ca

- The Lung Association, have a large area of their site devoted to those who wish to stop Smoking. Visit them at www.lung.ca/home-accueil_e.php

Excerpts from the Canadian Cancer Society Booklet

If you are a smoker, I hope the following excerpts from the Cancer Society booklet *For smokers who want to Quit* will encourage you to order one or more of their booklets to help you get started on a program to quit smoking. Information on how to order the booklets is provided at the end of this chapter. Not only do their booklets contain valuable information about the smoking problem, but they serve as an indispensable source of reference for anyone who wants to quit.

The following 10 excerpts are provided with permission from the Canadian Cancer Society, and I thank the Society for allowing me to print these excerpts in *Your Retirement Lifeline*. I hope you benefit from them.

1. Consider the benefits of quitting

No matter how long you've been smoking, your health will improve when you quit and your body will start to reverse some of the damage done by smoking. You'll see some changes right away and others as time goes on.

After your last cigarette:

- Within 20 minutes your blood pressure and pulse rate will return to normal.

- Within 8 hours you'll notice that you can breathe easier. Your oxygen levels will be back to normal and your chance of having a heart attack will go down.

- Within 24 hours your lungs will start to clear out the mucus. All that coughing will be a good sign.

- Within 48 hours you'll be nicotine free. Your senses of taste and smell will improve so you'll probably start to enjoy food more.

- Within 72 hours you'll have more energy. Your lung capacity will increase and your bronchial tubes will relax, so breathing and exercising will get easier.

- Within one year your risk of having a heart attack will drop by 50%.

- Within 10 years your risk of dying from lung cancer will be cut in half.

- Within 10 to 15 years your risk of coronary heart disease will be the same as the risk for someone who has never smoked.

2. Understand your options

People have successfully quit using many methods. There is no single way that works for everyone. You need to find the option that works best for you.

Quitlines

Every province and territory has a Quitline, where you can get free information on tobacco use and support to quit smoking.

You'll find your local Quitline number listed on the back of their booklet. Studies have shown that using a Quitline can double your chances of successfully quitting.

Quit aids

You can also try quit-smoking medicines. When used properly, many of these quit aids have been shown to increase your chances of successfully quitting.

Self-help guides

Self-help booklets (just like this one) are good tools to help you quit because they help you create a plan to follow. There are other great forms of self-help, such as online forums, interactive websites and Smartphone apps. Check out the app called Break It Off developed by the Canadian Cancer Society at cancer.ca/BreakItOffAPP

3. Nicotine replacement therapy (NRT)

Nicotine replacement therapy works by reducing the cravings caused by quitting smoking. It delivers a controlled dose of nicotine to your body over time. Each product is available in different doses so talk with your pharmacist or other healthcare professional about the correct dose for you.

NRT comes in 5 forms: patch, inhaler, oral spray, gum and lozenge. Each is available without a prescription at your drugstore, and the cost varies from approximately $4 to $8 a day. Although they all contain nicotine, they are much safer than tobacco and they don't cause cancer.

4. Set a quit date

Think about what's coming up over the next 30 days and pick a day to quit smoking. There may never be a perfect day to quit, but here are some things that might help you choose your date:

- Pick a day when your schedule is routine and nothing new is happening.

- Avoid dates where you have a deadline or something else that might distract you or give you additional stress.

- Make this your day for this task, so avoid other important dates like birthdays or anniversaries.

Share your date with your friends and family! Post it on Facebook or Twitter or send an email to let everyone know that you have taken this great step toward being smoke-free.

-5	-4	-3	-2	-1	0 Quit Date	+1	+2	+3	+4	+5

5. Prepare for your quit date

Now you know a bit about your triggers, why you want to quit and some of the things you'll face when you quit. Use the days leading up to your quit date to learn more about your smoking behaviours, like when, why and where you smoke and who you smoke with. At the back of this booklet, you'll find tracking cards (when you order a book the cards will be there) for you to start using at least 5 days before your quit date.)

Take the cards with you as you go through your day, and every time you have a cigarette, write it down on the card.

This is also an opportunity for you to try cutting back on the amount you smoke before your quit date. As you go through your day, look to see if there is a cigarette you can cut out – one that you can go without. If you do this every day, you might find yourself already halfway quit before you even start.

At the end of every day, take a moment to review your tracking card and see if you can pinpoint your triggers. The next day, try to use some of the coping strategies that you wrote in the triggers section to see if you can avoid a cigarette and get past the craving. Consider this a practice run. This is an opportunity for you to test out your plan before the big day.

6. On your quit day

You have worked hard to get here and you should be proud of yourself. Take a few moments to celebrate your positive decision to quit. It's not every day that you make a decision that will have such a big impact on the rest of your life.

Remember, though, that cravings can start at any time. When you feel yourself wanting a cigarette, do everything you can to get out of that situation and go somewhere else or do something else. Take control of your cravings.

Avoid people who are smoking

Do you usually have a cigarette with some of your co-workers during your break? Not today – head outside for a walk or take a break in the lunchroom with others.

Keep help within arm's reach

If you're taking NRT in the form of an inhaler, gum, a lozenge or a spray, keep it on hand and use it when you need to get through cravings.

Have your supports ready

Let the people around you know that you may reach out to them with a phone call or text. Keep your local Quitline number handy.

Take it easy

Quitting smoking is stressful enough on its own, so do what you can to remove yourself from other potentially stressful situations.

7. Stay fit and healthy

One of the main concerns people have when quitting smoking is a fear of gaining weight. About 1 in 5 people who quit smoking do not gain weight. For those who do gain weight, the average gain is about 5 to 10 pounds. Don't worry – there are ways to help ensure that any weight you gain is minimal.

Here are some helpful tips:

Stay active

Physical activity is a great way to help manage your weight and can also help with cravings and withdrawal symptoms. It's an investment in your health, and if you make it something enjoyable, you'll have a better chance of sticking to it.

Eat regularly

Don't skip meals. This can result in over-eating later in the day. It can also make you irritable, which may make it harder to resist cravings. Eat breakfast, lunch, dinner and 1 or 2 snacks every day.

Eat healthy snacks

Keep nutritious snacks prepared and ready for when you need them. Try raw veggies, fruit and Yogurt, and drink lots of water.

8. Deal with a slip

It's common to have a slip – take a puff or smoke a cigarette – after you quit smoking. If this happens, remember that a slip does not mean the end of your new smoke-free life. Think about how smoking makes you feel and focus on your reasons for quitting. Don't lose sight of your goal. One of these days, you will be smoke-free for good. Get back on track as soon as possible.

Here are some questions you can ask yourself to help you get back on track.

- What triggered you to have a cigarette or take a puff?
- Where were you?
- Who were you with?
- What can you do to avoid a slip the next time you are in this situation?

It's common to have a slip or two after you quit smoking. Remember that a setback doesn't mean you have to give up.

9. Live a smoke free life

Quitting is a challenge and you've succeeded so far. Your goal now is to make this change permanent and to continue living a smoke-free life.

Remember everything that you have learned and try not to become over-confident. Every day will bring new challenges and when you least expect it, a craving or trigger might throw you off.

Follow these tips to stay on track:

Reward yourself

Remember to celebrate the amazing job you're doing. Be grateful for your new smoke-free life.

Count on friends and family

Remind them that you still need their support! They've supported you all along and only want what is best for you.

Be prepared

Cravings and temptations can turn up at any time and you need to be ready to deal with them. Remember what has worked best for you so far.

Rely on tools

Keep their booklet nearby and use the tools and activities to help you stay on track. Call a Quitline or speak to your doctor, pharmacist or other healthcare provider if you need any additional support.

Once again, congratulations! You have joined the millions of Canadians who enjoy life without tobacco. Best wishes for your continued success and your new healthy lifestyle.

10. For more information

If you want to understand more about how people quit smoking, or you would like more information about the resources and programs in your community, call one of our information specialists toll-free at 1-888-

939-3333, email us at info@cis.cancer.ca or visit our website at cancer.ca.

Making Retirement Better

If you are a smoker, please take out your notebook and make a notation of what action you plan on taking that will make your retirement better.

Chapter 9

Peace of Mind When You Need It Most

As the house is cleaned, so the mind can be cleaned. As you enjoy a
clean house, you will enjoy a clean and uncluttered mind.

Source Unknown

R emez Sasson wrote the book 'Peace of Mind in Daily Life', so I
turned to him for a description of the title of this chapter. Here is
an excerpt in which he describes peace of mind. *(Reprinted with*
permission from Remez Sasson.)

"What is peace of mind? It is a state of inner calmness and tranquility,
together with a sense of freedom, when thoughts and worries cease, and
there is no stress, strain or fear. Such moments are not so rare. They
may be experienced while being engaged in some kind of an absorbing
or interesting activity, such as while watching an entertaining movie or
TV program, while being with someone you love, while reading a book
or while lying on the sand at the beach. Most people would be glad to
have some peace of mind in their life. They would be happy to forget
their troubles, problems and worries, and enjoy a few moments of inner
calmness and freedom from obsessing thoughts."

I don't expect this chapter to bring you the degree of 'inner calmness
and tranquility' that Ramez alludes to in his description, but I suspect
that this chapter, if heeded, will put a reasonable dent in your daily
worries.

Notice that Ramez says peace of mind may be experienced while being
engaged in some kind of absorbing activity. That same thought is
expressed in a previous chapter when we discussed the value of always
having a project underway.

Three Priorities

Retirement is a major milestone in your life, and a time when you need to view your life from a new perspective; especially your priorities. Having your priorities taken care of is exactly the type of thing that will bring you peace of mind. For instance, you have probably thought about getting your Last Will and Testament prepared but dismissed it as something you will attend to later at a more convenient time because there is no urgency right now. But if you have a heart attack tomorrow you would recognize it as a wakeup call and rush to get it done before week's end. Here are three documents that may require your attention without delay:

- Your Last Will & Testament

- Power of Attorney for Personal Care and Living Will

- Power of Attorney for Property

If you have already completed these documents, congratulations; but if not, you owe it to yourself and your family to attend to them. If you look after this chore now it will bring you Peace of Mind.

Your last Will & Testament

Your Will gives you control over how your money and property will be distributed after your death. Your Will allows you to ensure that certain people get particular parts of your estate. Since the law varies by province, all comments regarding Wills, Power of Attorney and Living Wills only apply to Ontario.

If you die without a Will

- Your estate will be distributed according to a government formula which may not coincide with your wishes.

- Your beneficiaries will incur additional costs before your estate is settled.

The Ontario Seniors Secretariat says this:

"Your will is the easiest and most effective way to tell others how you want your property and possessions– called your estate– to be distributed. Even if you don't have much money or property, it's still a good idea to have a will so you can name an executor and make it clear who you want making decisions after you die.

Under the law in most provinces and territories, your nearest relatives are the people who will share in your estate if you die without making a will. Depending how complicated your estate is, your relatives may need to hire a lawyer and go to court to deal with your estate. Sometimes, a government agency will get involved to make sure that your estate is dealt with properly."

In other words if you die without a will, the law will decide who the beneficiaries of your estate will be and what percentage each will receive. If you don't have a will, a government body will make the property distribution decision for you after your death and the results may not be what you wanted.

From recent surveys it appears that some 56% of Canadian adults have not completed their last will and testament. In the US that number is 65%. The most common reasons people give for being so lax about completing their will are: they feel they are still too young, they don't know how to get started; they feel it's too expensive, or they feel they do not have sufficient assets to warrant estate planning.

A phone call to a lawyer of your choice will give you an idea of the cost and possibly lead to getting your legal affairs in order before it's too late.

Not having a will can lead to a wide range of problems at a time when a family is already experiencing grief from the loss of a loved one. Belongings not going to the person they were intended for can lead to costly court battles and disruption within the family. Without a will, probate fees and other government charges typically far outweigh what you would pay an attorney to draft your will in the first place.

Years ago an elderly member of my family stubbornly refused to make a will despite the pleas of his immediate family. He stuck to his guns until the very end and died intestate, even though he owned his own home. It is my opinion that this gentleman felt that signing a will was akin to signing his own death warrant. No amount of logic would dissuade him from his stance; he seemed to believe that if he signed a will it would hasten his demise.

Is Your Will Current?

Your will should be updated whenever you or your family experience a major change in your life situation. Here are some of the events that could trigger the need for an update:

- A marriage or divorce

- Birth of a child

- Death of a family member

- Death of someone mentioned in your will

- A substantial change in the value of your estate

- Your executor is no longer able to serve

- You move to another province

Please go to the website of the Law Society of Upper Canada for additional information - www.lsuc.on.ca. From the home page of their website, click on 'For the Public', then 'Your Law', to arrive at a menu of choices including Wills and Estates. While at that site I highly recommend that you view the short video where two Ontario lawyers discuss the importance of having a properly drafted will and power of attorney.

Power of Attorney

A Power of Attorney is a legal document that authorizes another person, or an organization such as a trust company the right to act on your behalf. The word 'attorney' does not suggest that the person you select must be a lawyer. You may choose your spouse, a family member or a friend. For our purpose, we will discuss two commonly used Powers of Attorney documents:

- Power of Attorney for Personal Care and A Living Will

- Power of Attorney for Property

Power of Attorney for Personal Care

You will occasionally see a newspaper article describing someone who is being kept alive by artificial means; usually being demanded by a very determined relative. Such action usually occurs despite the protests of the hospital professional staff. One way to protect yourself from that type of situation is to have a Power of Attorney for Personal Care prepared well in advance.

That document provides you with an opportunity to choose someone you trust to act as your substitute decision-maker.

It is a way to ensure that the person acting on your behalf will make decisions that are in your best interests and similar to the decisions you would personally make. These decisions may include such items as your health care, clothing, housing, medical treatment, diet, hygiene and safety.

If you become ill and are unable to communicate your wishes, you will have peace of mind knowing that someone you trust is acting on your behalf. Power of Attorney for Personal Care also gives you an opportunity to state your specific wishes regarding certain medical treatments.

If you do not choose a substitute decision maker, the government may have to appoint someone to make certain decisions for you.

It is not legally necessary to engage a lawyer to prepare Powers of Attorney or a 'living will', but if your affairs are the least bit complicated it is a good idea to hire a lawyer to ensure that your documents are properly prepared.

To obtain a 'Power of Attorney Kit' published by the Office of the Public Guardian and Trustee call toll-free at 1-800-366-0335. The

Office of the Public Guardian and Trustee (OPGT) is part of Ontario's Ministry of the Attorney General.

The 'Community Legal Education Ontario' provides a comprehensive reference website at www.cleo.on.ca/en.

A Living Will

A 'living will' is a document that only addresses your treatment and personal care wishes. If you have a lawyer prepare a Power of Attorney for Personal Care, your 'living will' statement becomes an integral part of your Power of Attorney for Personal Care document.

Here is a description from the website of the Ontario Ministry of the Attorney General.

'The expression "living will" is sometimes used to refer to a document in which you write down what you want to happen if you become ill and can't communicate your wishes about treatment. It is quite common, for example, for people to write a "living will" saying that they do not want to be kept alive on artificial life supports if they have no hope of recovery. The term "advance directive" is also frequently used to refer to such a document. Some people use the phrase "proxy directive" to describe a document that combines a Power of Attorney and a living will".

Example

Here is an excerpt showing the main thrust of my own Living Will.

If a situation arises in which there is no reasonable expectation of my own recovery from an extreme physical or mental disability and my death is otherwise imminent, I request the following:

- *I want all possible pain medication during a terminal illness.*

- *I do not want to be resuscitated to a diminished quality of life where I will be totally dependent on others for personal care.*

- *I do not want to be kept alive by any artificial means or life support.*

Power of Attorney for Property

When you give someone of your choosing, Power of Attorney for Property that person will have the legal authority to make financial decisions for you if you are unable to do so. That person will be able to act on your behalf in financial dealings, such as banking, buying or selling real estate, and buying everyday personal needs.

Unless you limit that person's authority, he or she can do almost anything with your property that you could do. However, that person cannot make or change your will, or give a new Power of Attorney on your behalf.

If you become unable to make financial decisions on your own, and have not appointed anyone to act on your behalf through a Power of Attorney for Property, the Government or the Court will choose someone for you. As you can see, someone with Power of Attorney has almost unlimited control over your assets, so it is most important that you to select that person with care, and the guidance of a lawyer.

Prearranged Funeral & Cemetery Services

My wife Olga and I prearranged our funerals and paid for them about ten years ago. As someone once said, 'this is one trip you know you are going to make', so why not prepare for it ahead of time. We have never regretted our decision and it has brought 'peace of mind' to us and our family. We know that everything has been arranged according to our wishes and our family know that when we die they will not be faced with tough last minute decisions at a time when they are grieving the loss of a parent.

Initially we were somewhat apprehensive about turning over thousands of dollars in prepayment for two funerals, but we soon learned that prepaid funds are protected by a Compensation Fund which is funded by all funeral homes and administered by the Board of Funeral Services, the regulatory body in the Province of Ontario.

If you meet with a funeral director to discuss a prearranged funeral you will get answers to all of your questions related to costs and services.

You also will be able to make unhurried decisions regarding the type of casket you want, the funeral service itself, your burial preference, and entombment or cremation.

A number of nursing homes now require that funeral arrangements are in place before entering their home.

To me, a prearranged funeral makes perfect sense.

- You will have peace of mind in knowing that your wishes will be met at the time of your death.

- Your family will be pleased to know that they will not be required to attend to last minute decisions at a time when they are ill prepared to make good decisions. They may also be pleased to know they don't have to pick up the bill.

- By prepaying for your funeral, you have in effect locked in the funeral cost at the time of payment. Below is an excerpt from a letter I received from my funeral home after we prearranged our funeral:

    "The (name) Funeral Home prearrangement as described in our contract #------ with you is guaranteed. This means that the investment funds allocated to these charges will always be considered sufficient. Therefore, your estate will never be asked for additional funds to cover these items."

Prearranging for your Cemetery and related services is much the same as arranging for your funeral. Many new cemeteries are opening up so there are plenty of locations to choose from. If there is a possibility that you may move to another city later in life be sure to check out their transfer policy, and if acceptable, get it in writing.

A Useful Website

Here is the website for the Ontario Seniors Secretariat.

www.seniors.gov.on.ca/en/index.php.

Once you visit this site you will see that it is a most useful resource for anyone living in retirement. Their sole purpose is to meet the needs of seniors and help them lead active, healthy lives. Through their site they keep seniors informed about programs and services, healthy lifestyles and aging.

Living Alone

With increased longevity and women living 83.3 years compared to men at 78.8 years, it follows that women will live alone longer than men.

You may be surprised to learn from Statistics Canada that 43% of Canadians over the age of 65 are single. And that on average a Canadian woman loses her spouse at age 56, not in old age. However, at age 65 women are three times as likely to be widowed as their 65 year old male counterpart.

Women will be pleased to hear this from Nikki Lively, a staff therapist at the Family Institute at Northwestern University. "Older women are usually more content (than men) with taking care of their own needs after the death of a spouse." But she also commented that, "While relishing their independence, older women still go through various levels of loneliness."

Probably the most helpful thing to leave you with is the following website addresses which you can explore for information and support.

- Widowed.ca is a Canada's only free online resource for widows, widowers and their loved ones, providing an easy way to locate a wide variety of information and services needed after the loss of a loved one.

- The Mayo Clinic at www.mayoclinic.com.

- The Medicine Net at www.medicinenet.com/script/main/hp.asp.

- The Toronto Grace Centre, Toronto at www.torontograce.org.

Simplify Your Life

Once the kids have left the nest, thousands of seniors decide to sell their big house with the four bedrooms and buy something smaller, that will be easier to clean and less costly to maintain.

Others take it a step further and move into a condo because it gives them more freedom to come and go as they please. Somehow this whole process became known as downsizing.

Once you reach retirement age there is a natural tendency to rid yourself of certain responsibilities, habits and practices that no longer contribute to your well being. I wholeheartedly support the trend; why continue to do something out of habit when it no longer serves any purpose in your retirement lifestyle? This is a time when you should streamline your life to make it more relaxed and pleasurable.

There are scores of situations in life which can seriously hamper our ability to achieve peace of mind. Sometimes these circumstances are beyond our control, but not all. You must clarify in your own mind exactly what type of life you want. Then you must decide to do those things you enjoy, not what others think you should do. You must learn to say 'no' and not feel guilty about it.

Here are some ways to simplify your life. You may be able to identify with most.

- Simplify your life by eliminating certain activities and responsibilities that create stress and unpleasantness in your life.

- If you have constant conflict with an acquaintance, friend or relative reduce or eliminate contact with that person.

- Do you attend a certain event such as bingo, the casino, the theatre, or poker night, out of a sense of duty or because someone else expects you to. If you do attend certain functions but would prefer not to, you owe it to yourself to muster up the courage to stop that practice. Find something more enjoyable to do during that time, and then let people know about the new interest in your life.

- Cultivate relationships with people who make you feel good. Limit or avoid contact with people who cause you stress.

- I know a grandmother who is overworked and exhausted from babysitting three small grandchildren for her two sons who both have good paying jobs and could easily afford to pay for regular day care. The two sons are oblivious to their mother's plight, and since the mother feels it is her duty to care for the grandchildren she suffers in silence. Don't let that happen to you – speak up.

- Acquire spiritual beliefs that give you inner peace and a sense of contentment, not guilt.

- If something is troubling you do your best to deal with it. The disturbing issue may be family related, something financial, a health matter or even spiritual; whatever it is, don't let it continue unresolved for the rest of your life. Attend to it, and the wretched thing will, like a fog, vanish from your mind

Reduce the Clutter

When you move into your new downsized location, the first thing that will hit you is, "Where did all the space go?" The only way to recover your lost space is to get rid of stuff. I refer to books, clothes, dishes, old TV's, and everything else that no longer fits your new lifestyle. Dispose of family heirlooms to your children; that's the natural progression anyway, from you to your children. Give what's left over to Goodwill or the Salvation Army. Reduce the clutter and simplify your life.

From now on, whenever you buy something new, dispose of whatever was replaced. If you buy a new television or computer, don't store the old one in your locker room or the basement just in case someone may want it a decade from now. Dispose of it now and gain that peace of mind.

Make Use of Technology

If you constantly worry about having to get to the bank to make your monthly Visa payment on time, dispense with that worry and arrange for

Visa to make automatic withdrawals from your bank account each month. While you are at it why not arrange for automatic payment of all your regular bills such as property taxes, car payments, insurance payments and so forth.

Even President Obama is trying to simplify his life by reducing the number of decisions he has to make each day. "You'll notice I wear only grey or blue suits", he told Vanity Fair magazine. He said he does not want to make decisions about what he 'eats' or what he 'wears', because he has too many other decisions to make throughout the day.

Get a Pet

Pets provide peace of mind and companionship to millions of Canadians every day. There is no doubt about it; pets help beat depression and loneliness. Most of our friends have a dog or cat; we have a cat. Sure, a pet requires care and attention but in return they give you their undivided love and affection.

If you are considering getting a pet, I caution you to look into exactly how much attention a pet requires on a daily basis. There is also a cost for food, veterinary visits and other incidentals. And remember, if you intend to vacation for a period of time each year, you will need to arrange for boarding, either with a place like Pet's Mart or a friend or neighbour.

Making Retirement Better

If you have not attended to the important legal matters discussed in this chapter I urge you to do so without delay as this is your last chance. If there is anything else you intend to do that will increase your peace of mind and make your retirement better enter your thoughts in your special notebook now.

This would be an opportune time to summarize on one or more sheets of paper, the notes you made at the end of each chapter. That way you will have a convenient source of reference you can turn to from time to time when you want to recall what you planned to do to make your retirement better.

Closing Thoughts

I would like to leave you with three closing thoughts.

- A message about stress.
- Dr. Rubin's observations about happiness.
- A personal note.

Stress (Author Unknown)

A young lady confidently walked around the room while she explained stress management to an audience; with a raised glass of water, and everyone knew she was going to ask the ultimate question, 'half empty or half full?'..... She fooled them all... "How heavy is this glass of water?" she inquired with a smile. Answers called out ranged from 8 oz. to 20 oz.

She replied, "The absolute weight doesn't matter. It depends on how long I hold it. If I hold it for a minute, that's not a problem. If I hold it for an hour, I'll have an ache in my right arm. If I hold it for a day, you'll have to call an ambulance. In each case it's the same weight, but the longer I hold it, the heavier it becomes."

She continued, "And that's the way it is with stress. If we carry our burdens all the time, sooner or later, as the burden becomes increasingly heavy, we won't be able to carry on."

"As with the glass of water, you have to put it down for a while and rest before holding it again. When we're refreshed, we can carry on with the burden - holding stress longer and better each time practiced. So, as early in the evening as you can, put all your burdens down. Don't carry them through the evening and into the night.... pick them up tomorrow. Whatever burdens you're carrying now, put them down for a moment. Relax; pick them up later after you've rested. Life is short. Enjoy it and the now 'supposed' stress that you've conquered!"

Are You Happy?

When we discuss Quality of Life in the opening chapter of this book we were dabbling with that feeling we call 'happiness'. Since they are close cousins so to speak, I want to acquaint you with Dr. Theodore Rubin's observations about happiness.

Dr. Rubin says that happiness consists of feeling good, being relatively free of anxiety. It is not exhilaration or highs of any kind. He says that if you are feeling good, almost everything you encounter has some pleasurable aspect. There are a great number of people who are happy, but since they don't know they are happy, they are not happy. He makes the point that in our society most of us have all the necessities and a great deal more. If a person from a less prosperous country could live the way we live, they would certainly be happy. Thus if happiness is to come, it will not come from anything additional, from the outside. It must come from a rearrangement of how we perceive ourselves. We have to redefine what we call happiness, and what it is we want.

Dr. Rubin points out that if you are doing something you enjoy, which gives you satisfaction, the doing is more important than the accomplishment. The process of writing a book or working on a project can be exciting, and when the book or project is finished you feel another kind of satisfaction. However, if the end result was your only satisfaction and the process was looked upon with disdain and contempt, you would miss out on all the time and energy you put into writing the book or completing the project. He concludes that since the process of what you do lasts much longer than the end result you should enjoy the process of whatever you do.

A Personal Note

Thank you for reading Your Retirement Lifeline. Over the years I have learned from firsthand experience what factors are of greatest significance during these final years. I wrote this book so that I could pass on some of what I have learned, to the younger generations. I do hope you found information and inspiration that will help make your retirement better.

I have now reached the age of ninety, and I would like to leave you with this thought. Whatever changes you need to make to your lifestyle; whether it is losing weight, getting into better physical condition, eating healthier foods, reducing the stress in your life, managing your finances better, or injecting more fun into your life, now is the time to begin making those changes. Not next week or at a more convenient time.

Here's why; your lifestyle in your 50's will determine your quality of life when you reach 60. Your lifestyle during your 60's will determine your quality of life when you reach 70, and the cycle repeats itself for as long as you live. Whatever your age, you should actively do your very best to achieve the highest quality of life possible for your circumstances; and who knows, this may become the best years of your life.

I wish you well and trust that you will enjoy success and happiness in the years ahead.

###